Beppe Porcheddu

Beppe Porcheddu

Soldier, Artist and Partisan

David Ross

THE CHOIR PRESS

Published privately in the United Kingdom in 2021

This edition published in the United Kingdom in 2024 by
The Choir Press

ISBN 978-1-78963-445-7

To Jacqui, Antonia, James, Jonathan and all the family,
so that you may know something more of
this remarkable man

Contents

Preface

I never knew my grandfather, Giuseppe Porcheddu, known as Beppe, but he visited me shortly after I was born, in November 1947. He was accompanied by his wife, my grandmother, Margarita (Rita). My father Michael Ross and my mother Giovanna, the daughter of Beppe and Rita, were living in Austria at the time, where my father, a serving British Army officer, was working with the United Nations War Crimes Commission.

Beppe was a well-known Italian artist, and he brought with him a painting he had completed depicting an angel returning a toy to a child's bedroom. It was a gift for me, and I still have the painting.

Shortly after visiting my parents, Beppe returned to Italy alone to prepare for an exhibition of his paintings in Rome. On 27 December 1947, whilst in Rome, Beppe disappeared. His passport and walking stick, without which he could not walk far, were still in his room. He was never to be seen again.

This extraordinary and inexplicable tragedy was to cast a long shadow over my family. My mother and grandmother spoke very little about my grandfather as I grew up. Perhaps it was still all too raw for them.

Eventually, stories about Beppe emerged: of his family and upbringing, his precocious artistic talent, his near-death as an eighteen-year-old volunteer officer in the Italian Alpine troops fighting the Austrians and Germans, his temporary exile from Italy as a result of his anti-fascism, his work in support of the partisans and his harbouring of British escaped prisoners of war. He became an accomplished and well-known artist and was also much sought after as an illustrator of children's books. He was knighted before the rise of Mussolini for his contribution to the arts. One wonders what more he might have achieved in life had he not disappeared at the age of forty-nine.

In writing this biography of Beppe I have relied on accounts from the family and their friends. Much has already been written on Beppe as an artist, but little is known about his anti-fascism and support of the partisans. My father in his war memoir, *From Liguria with Love*, which was reprinted in 2019 under the new title of *The British Partisan*, writes of Beppe and the risks he took sheltering him and another British officer. Yet Beppe remains unknown in so many ways.

Following the death of my father in 2012 and my mother in 2019, and acting as executor to their wills, I went through many family papers which had remained undisturbed for many years. Many were to prove invaluable in providing timelines and important information, and were to shed light into the dark corners of Beppe Porcheddu's life and his character.

Beppe lived through the momentous times of the first half of the twentieth century, which was dominated by two world wars. In writing about Beppe I have attempted to describe the times in which he lived. Events undoubtedly shaped his character and influenced his decision-making. His experiences and character can also be seen in his art, which has received critical acclaim, and even more so since his disappearance in 1947.

I have indicated in the footnotes all the sources I have drawn on as background to put Beppe's life in the context of the events of the time. In studying the background and history of the times in which he lived, every effort has been made to attribute all sources correctly. Where I have failed, it has not been for a lack of effort. If at times I have provided more information than might be considered necessary, I felt that these were indeed extraordinary times and undoubtedly had a profound effect on Beppe, which may perhaps eventually provide a clue with regard to his disappearance. A bibliography is included at the end.

I am indebted to many members of my family for providing stories about Beppe and sharing their views on his character. These were essential in writing about someone I did not know. I am particularly grateful to my late father, mother and grandmother, who have been my primary sources since my childhood. As so often happens, I failed to ask them all the questions I would have liked answers to whilst they were alive.

Of invaluable help has been my wife Jacqui. She proofread my drafts and spotted my many errors. Additionally, she improved all the photographs and images and prepared them for printing. My thanks also go to my sister, Alessandra Alexandroff, who provided information on Beppe and, being herself an accomplished artist, gave me valuable comments on Beppe's art as well as help with proofreading. To Emanuele Ertola of Pavia University who obtained Beppe's war service records. Finally, my Canadian cousin, Vivianne Vallarino, whose mother was my mother's twin sister and who also provided information on Beppe.

Beppe Porcheddu led a rich and colourful life. He put his life in danger many times, and eventually it took its toll. He was an enigma in so many ways, and his story deserves to be told.

CHAPTER I

Early Family Life and
Artistic Beginnings

Giuseppe Porcheddu, better known as Beppe, was born in Turin, Italy, on 1 May 1898. The year was marked by riots all over Italy as a result of a shortage of bread. The year before had seen a very low wheat harvest, and imported grain was more expensive as a result of the Spanish–American War of 1898. Wheat prices increased, and the abolition of duty on imported wheat was too little and too late.

Young Beppe, as a result of his privileged upbringing, was unaffected by these events, but a peaceful life it was not to be. Beppe was to be at the heart of two momentous world wars, nearly losing his life in the first as an officer serving with the Alpini, and escaping imprisonment and execution in the second as an anti-fascist. He deserved a quiet retirement, but that also eluded him in the most dramatic way.

His home city of Turin is the capital city of the region of Piedmont in northern Italy. The city is famous for its architecture, history and culture. David Gilmour, in his book *The Pursuit of Italy*,[1] describes the city, much of which dates back to the sixteenth and eighteenth centuries. From 1563 Turin was the capital of the Duchy of Savoy, then of the Kingdom of Sardinia ruled by the House of Savoy. It was the first Italian capital from 1861 to 1865.

In the mid-nineteenth century Piedmont was considered the most progressive Italian state, prosperous and liberal, the only one capable of leading a brave new Italy. In fact it was emerging as the great European hope of British liberals and directly the opposite of Naples. It is interesting to note that, in 1860, the whole of southern Italy had only 125 miles of railway track, whilst Piedmont had over 600.

During Beppe's life Turin was a major European political centre. Previously, it had played an important part in the unification of Italy known as the Risorgimento, which was completed in 1871.

---

[1] David Gilmour, *The Pursuit of Italy* (London: Penguin, 2012)

Gilmour goes on to review where Italy is today. He writes that, after World War II, Italy was divided into regions recognising the country's historical traditions, and some were granted substantial autonomy to neutralise separatist demands.

In the 1980s dissatisfaction with the inefficiencies of central government led to the formation of the Lombard League. Support for the movement increased, and it was renamed the Northern League and became an electoral force. The appeal of the League was mainly economic, resenting high taxes, mismanagement by the government in Rome and 'allowing corrupt and idle southerners to live beyond their means'.[2]

Although the 'Torinese' of today remain fiercely independent and are proud of their education, culture and economic progress, one wonders what Beppe would have made of modern-day Italy. Support for separatism of some form has continued to this day, and the unrest seen in 2017 is unlikely to abate.

Turin's artistic heritage and liberal views may have had an important influence on the young Beppe, but there was no feeling of arrogance or superiority in his character. In fact, quite the opposite. He was born into a

Turin, the birthplace of Beppe Porcheddu and all of his family. The capital of the Piedmont region, famous for its architecture, history and culture.

---

[2] Ibid.

wealthy family. His father Giovanni Antonio Porcheddu (1860–1937), however, was brought up in poverty in Sardinia, having been orphaned from an early age.

Gaining a number of scholarships, Giovanni went on to become a highly successful engineer and the first in Italy to realise that the future of construction lay in the reinforcement of concrete with steel rods. This technique was invented by the Belgian engineer François Hennebique (1842–1921). With great foresight, and not without considerable personal and professional risk, Giovanni Porcheddu obtained the patent for this new technique for Italy and went on to form

Giovanni Porcheddu (1860–1937), Beppe's father, who rose from poverty in Sardinia to become one of the most famous and successful civil engineers in Italy.

a highly successful construction company bearing his name. The company was to become responsible for over 2,600 constructions throughout Italy over a period of thirty years. A publication by Riccardo Nelva and Bruno Signorelli[3] studied the work of Giovanni and his use of this technique.

Amongst Giovanni's most important constructions, many of which still stand today, are the grain silos of the Port of Genoa built between 1899 and 1901, which at the time were the largest reinforced concrete structures in the world. The building that houses the silos is in a prominent position, particularly when seen from the sea at the entrance of the bay. As a warehouse for grain it was still functioning until the beginnings of the 1990s, and it was a key element in the transformation of the waterfront masterminded by Renzo Piano, the famous architect who also designed the Shard in London. In 2019 the historical and architectural importance of the building was recognised by the Western Ligurian Sea Port Authority and tenders were invited to redevelop it.

---

[3] Riccardo Nelva and Bruno Signorelli, *Avvento ed evoluzione del calcestruzzo armato in Italia: il Sistema Hennebique* (Milan: AITEC, 1990)

The grain silos of the port of Genova. Built by Giovanni between 1899 and 1901, and at the time the largest reinforced structures in the world. Today, the buildings and the area are being transformed by the famous architect Renzo Piano.

Another of his more important constructions was the iconic Fiat factory at Lingotto, Turin, with its car racecourse on the roof immortalised in the car chase in the film *The Italian Job*, starring Michael Caine. Construction started in 1916 and the building opened in 1923. At the time of its construction it was the largest car factory in the world. Fiat, run by Giovanni Agnelli, who was a close friend of Porcheddu, was to become the third largest company in Italy, having prospered greatly from supplying army vehicles for World War I.

Il Lingotto, Turin. The Fiat factory constructed by Giovanni, with the iconic race track on the roof. Construction started in 1916 and the factory was opened in 1923. Renzo Piano redeveloped the factory, retaining the race track.

The Lingotto factory was finally closed in 1982, and Piano redeveloped the factory into a modern complex of shopping arcades, concert halls, a hotel and a convention centre. The racecourse has been retained and can be visited.

Giovanni constructed several bridges over Italy's major rivers, including the Risorgimento Bridge in Rome over the Tiber, which was built in 1911. The bridge has an arch span of 100 metres, with no central support, and at the time became the world's longest reinforced concrete bridge. Many were highly sceptical of its construction and said it would collapse, but the bridge still stands today. As if to demonstrate his confidence in the bridge Giovanni, accompanied by the young Beppe, sat in a boat underneath the bridge to observe the removal of the wooden supports after the concrete had set.

The Risorgimento Bridge over the Tiber in Rome. Completed in 1911, and at the time the longest single span bridge in the world.

The opening of the bridge became a major occasion, with a military procession accompanying the king, Victor Emmanuel III. At the opening the king remarked to Giovanni, 'I may be the king of Italy, but you are the king of construction.'

Giovanni also built the new bell tower of St Mark's Basilica in St Mark's Square, Venice, following the collapse of the original in 1902. The tower is 98.6 metres tall and is an exact replica of the original. It was completed in 1912 on St Mark's feast day, exactly 1,000 years after the foundations of the original are thought to have been laid. Smaller replicas have been built in many countries. Galileo demonstrated his telescope to the Doge of Venice on 21 August 1609 from the campanile, as the bell tower is known in Italian.

Beppe was to take a great interest in his father's work and from an early

St Mark's Square, Venice, and the remains of the campanile (bell tower), which collapsed in 1902. Galileo demonstrated his telescope to the Doge of Venice from it on 21 August 1609.

Giovanni rebuilt the campanile as an exact replica of the original. It was completed in 1912, exactly 1,000 years after the foundations of the original are thought to have been laid.

age was able to observe both architecture and engineering in action.

Beppe was brought up by his father to appreciate both architecture and art, and with a freedom of ideas and expression. Giovanni instilled in Beppe a respect for all people, irrespective of background, and a clear sense of right and wrong.

Beppe was to lead a very rich and colourful life, but not without considerable challenges and personal risk. He was to become a famous illustrator of books, particularly those for children, a ceramist and painter. From the 1920s to the 1940s he became recognised as one of the finest illustrators in Italy. His artistic talents led him to explore other media and he became a highly successful sculptor as well as a designer of ceramics, dolls, furniture and toys for Lenci.

Beppe was the fourth of seven children. His brothers were Mario and Luciano and his sisters Eugenia, Teresa, Ambrogia and Amalia. A number of his siblings were also talented artists and Eugenia became a successful writer of children's books, for which he became her illustrator.

Beppe was brought up in privileged circumstances in a vast family villa in Via Ormea, a street in the centre of Turin. His schooling was conducted entirely in Turin and after school he entered the Polytechnic of Turin, graduating with a degree in architecture. He was to become particularly attached to the city and was invited to design a number of civic awards and diplomas. He was an enthusiastic sportsman and a Greek and Latin scholar as well as an accomplished violinist. His love of music, the classics and art were to have an indelible and profound influence on his art and on his family in the years to come.

Despite having a degree in architecture and a father with a successful construction company, Beppe did not follow in his father's career path. From a very early age his artistic talent became apparent, so much so that

Beppe (second on the left in front) and his siblings. Turin, 1901.

Beppe dressed for his first Holy Communion. Turin, 1910.

the famous sculptor Leonardo Bistolfi, who also had his own school of sculpture, immediately recognised Beppe's talent. As a close friend of Beppe's father, Bistolfi was a frequent visitor to the family home in Turin. On one such visit in 1905 he was almost in disbelief upon seeing the maturity in the art of the seven-year-old Beppe. Bistolfi was later to write an extensive introduction to and critical analysis of Beppe's paintings.[4]

Initially, Beppe was self-taught in art. He was inspired towards developing his prodigious talent after attending the first International Exhibition of Humour in Italy, held in Rivoli in 1911 when he was aged thirteen. In the same year one of his sketches was published in the *Corriere dei Piccoli*, a popular publication for children to which he would contribute many illustrations both as a boy and as an adult; he also contributed illustrations to the *Domenica dei Fanciulli*. He took much of his artistic inspiration from illustrators such as Arthur Rackham and Edmund Dulac, and the family still has an extensive library of books illustrated by Rackham and Dulac which have inspired successive generations as they did Beppe.

Following classical studies and encouraged by Bistolfi, Beppe attended drawing classes in the Faculty of Architecture of the Politecnico di Torino.

Life could not have been better for the young Beppe: a talented scholar and artist, surrounded by members of a successful and affluent family, who lacked for nothing. On 28 June 1914, however, Archduke Franz Ferdinand of Austria and his wife were assassinated in Sarajevo by Gavrilo Princip, a nineteen-year-old member of Young Bosnia, a revolutionary movement pursuing unification into a Yugoslavia. The Archduke was the heir presumptive to the throne of Austria-Hungary. His assassination led to Austria-Hungary's declaration of war against Serbia, which in turn triggered a series of events that would lead eventually to Austria-Hungary's allies and Serbia's allies declaring war on each other, thus starting World War I. The artistic development of the young Beppe would now be delayed.

---

[4] Leonardo Bistolfi, *Disegni di Giuseppe Porcheddu* (Turin, 1928)

CHAPTER II

Italy Enters World War I,
Beppe Volunteers

At the start of World War I Italy remained neutral, watching develop-ments carefully. Italy had two longstanding enemies, both on its borders: France and Austria. Italy's dilemma was where to build its defences, as it expected to enter the conflict at some stage, but on whose side?

In early 1915 Austria, encouraged by Germany, offered territorial concessions to Italy to induce it to remain neutral. Austria was willing to give up Trento and most of the surrounding province, which had always been disputed territory with Italy. Additionally, Trieste would become an autonomous region and Austria would withdraw from other disputed areas, allowing an Italian occupation. In the secret Treaty of London, however, the Allies promised Italy Trieste, southern Tyrol, northern Dalmatia and other territories in return for entering the war on the side of the Allies.

Despite the opposition of most Italians, who favoured neutrality, Italy joined the war against Austria-Hungary in May 1915. Italy had decided the Allies had the better prospects and siding with them would be far more valuable to its national interests in terms of territorial gains. It was, however, another sixteen months before Italy declared war on Germany.

The Italian king at the time was Victor Emmanuel III. He had acceded to the throne following the assassination of his father, Umberto I, in 1900 by an anarchist who wanted to avenge those killed in Milan during the bread riots of 1898.

Victor Emmanuel III became known as the 'Soldier King' as he was to reign until 1946, through both world wars, prior to being forced into exile. The decisions the king made between 1915 and 1946 were disastrous for his country and led to the end of his dynasty and of the monarchy. He committed Italy to two world

The Italian king Victor Emmanuel III (1869–1947), who reigned during both world wars.

wars that were unpopular with the majority of his people. Between the wars, in 1922, he refused his own government's request to impose martial law, which might have prevented Mussolini's rise to power. The monarchy was replaced by the Italian Republic after the constitutional referendum held on 2 June 1946.

Italy began the war against Austria-Hungary along Italy's northern border, including high up in what are now the Italian Alps and along the Isonzo river. The first shells were fired in the dawn of 24 May 1915 against the enemy positions of Cervignano del Friuli, which was captured a few hours later. The Italian commander-in-chief was General Luigi Cadorna, who favoured frontal assaults and whose tactics were to cost the lives of hundreds of thousands of Italians.

The future fascist leader Benito Mussolini was serving as a corporal in the army and was involved in action on the Isonzo. He was wounded three times during the war. The final time was on 22 February 1917, when the accidental explosion of a mortar bomb killed four Italian soldiers but only wounded Sergeant Mussolini. He was to spend six months in hospital having shrapnel extracted. After his discharge from hospital Mussolini returned to journalism, which became the platform for his political career.

General Cadorna (1850–1928), who was Italian commander at the beginning of World War I. Buried in Bordighera, where he lived in retirement.

On 4 August 1916 Cadorna launched another offensive on the Isonzo. The previous five offensives by the Italians on the river had been largely unsuccessful. This time, however, the Italian artillery made the difference as Cadorna had managed to bring up 1,200 artillery pieces. After an initial bombardment, the Italians advanced and captured Gorizia at the foot of the Alps on the Slovene border. Cadorna was unable to exploit this success as the Austrian's second defensive line held. The Italians had suffered over 50,000 casualties to add to the 220,000 previously suffered in the first five battles on the Isonzo.[5] The Italian army, despite the heavy losses, was improving its war

---

[5] Background reading: Mark Thompson, *The White War: Life and Death on the Italian Front 1915–1919* (London: Faber, 2008)

fighting capability, which was to serve it well in the latter part of the war.

In the meantime Italy continued to trade with the Allies' principal enemy, Germany. Large sections of the population and parliament were opposed to the war and could have no idea of the losses the Italians would suffer in a conflict that would last much longer than anyone had imagined. The objective for Italy was to regain Tyrol and Trieste, but nearly three quarters of a million Italians were to die. Many were killed in the Dolomite Alps in the most harsh and unforgiving environment.

Beppe's artistic studies were cut short as, despite his passion for art, Beppe alone amongst his brothers decided he must join the war effort. He volunteered for army service and was selected for officer training. For him defeating the Austrians, who were claiming much of Italian South Tyrol, was enough of an incentive to volunteer and to go to war. One can but imagine what his family thought at the time, as conscription had yet to be implemented.

He undertook his officer training at the Italian Military Academy at Modena. A pass dated July 1917 records Beppe as leaving the academy for weekend leave. The original academy dates back to 1756 under the Duchy of Milan. In 1798, Napoleon Bonaparte expanded the academy's curriculum to include a military engineering school and artillery school, and it trained all army officers in Italy until 1814.

On commissioning, Beppe took no soft option and applied to join the Alpini. The Alpini were established in 1872, shortly after the unification of Italy. They were originally raised to defend Italy's borders with France and the Austro-Hungarian empire. During World War I there were eighty-eight battalions. These were specialised mountain troops, skilled in climbing and skiing, and were a logical choice for the young Beppe, who was only eighteen at the time. He loved the mountains above Turin from where the regiment recruited. He was also fit, athletic and a skier.

He joined the Pinerolo Battalion of the 3rd Regiment of Alpini as a Second Lieutenant in August 1917. The regiment had been formed on 1 November 1882, and it originally consisted of three battalions named after the valleys from

Soldiers of the Alpini Regiment with a mortar. Beppe was an officer in the 3rd Regiment, fighting the Austrians and Germans.

where the soldiers were recruited: Val Stura, Val Maira and Monti Lessini. During World War I the regiment had thirteen battalions, and today the regiment consists of one battalion, Susa, and is based in Pinerolo, in the province of Turin. In 2007 it was deployed to Kabul, Afghanistan, as part of the International Security Assistance Force (ISAF), the NATO-led security force in Afghanistan.

It is not known why Beppe was selected for officer training, but perhaps his education, character and fitness set him apart from many of the other volunteers.

The 3rd Regiment of Alpini was deployed on the Monte Grappa massif and formed part of 51,000 Italian troops. Facing the Alpini were 120,000 Austrians and Germans. The massif represented vital ground as it covered the left flank of the Italian Piave front. It was into this front that Beppe was to be deployed.

The Great War Society[6] records that, much as Verdun or Gallipoli, the attrition on Monte Grappa embodied the Great War. This battlefield is rarely mentioned and has a quality that makes its story particularly dramatic. Imagine the Somme with a 2,000-foot elevation gain for every mile. Or imagine Ypres having forty-degree rock slopes with trenches chiselled out of solid stone. A high rate of casualties was typical of World War I battles, but here the attackers had to advance up mountain slopes, over barren rock, in dense cloud and howling wind or in a horizontal blizzard of sleet or snow. The resilience and tactical effectiveness of the Italian infantrymen and the troops of the crumbling Austro-Hungarian empire stand out amongst the great engagements of World War I.

Mark Thompson, in his book *The White War*, explains that the Austrians aimed to capture the eastern and western flanks of Monte Grappa and contain the Italian fortress dug in under the summit. The southwestern ridge, Monte Asolone, was a crucial target, as it would enable the Austrian and German forces to cut off the supply road to the Italian fort. Supplies and wounded fighters were also transported by cable cars across the front.

The goal to the southeast was Monte Tomba, the name aptly meaning 'tomb', and it was here that Beppe and the 3rd Alpini were dug in in defensive positions. Each of the four Alpini companies that would have made up a battalion would have been responsible for a particular sector of the defensive line. The companies would have been positioned so that they could support each other with heavy machine guns trained to fire across the

---

[6] Rich Galli, *Monte Grappa: Italy's Thermopylae* (Great War Society)

front of their neighbouring defensive positions. This is called enfilade fire and is considered the most effective way of cutting down advancing infantry.

Within each company there would have been probably three or four platoons with thirty infantrymen in each. The platoons would have been dug in on the front line, occupying a trench system that would have taken several days or even weeks to prepare.

The men would live, eat and rest in these trenches. In front of the trenches razor-sharp wire would have been laid out. This was designed to slow an enemy advance and also channel the attackers onto ground covered by machine guns and artillery. The trenches would have had overhead cover to give some protection against aerial bombardments as some of the enemy shells would have been primed to explode in the air, sending shrapnel over the trenches. Other shells might be designed with delayed fuses so that the shell embedded itself in the rocky ground before exploding, thus magnifying its effect.

The front line was clearly not a pleasant place to be, but at least the trench system gave some protection to the defender, unlike the attacking troops, who would have been out in the open.

Both the attackers and defenders would have been supported by artillery, including mortars, which were able to fire shells on a very high trajectory from a relatively short range and were ideal for mountain warfare. They would have been positioned behind the front line and were able to fire over the peaks and mountains. The defenders would have identified the most likely areas where the attackers might group or form up before an attack and these positions would have been 'registered', with each target area allocated its own number. Forward observation officers were able to see the impact areas and could make any necessary adjustments by relaying instructions to the artillery using an extensive telephone network, so that fire could be brought to bear exactly where and when it was required.

The same network of communication cables also allowed the Alpini companies to keep in contact with each other. That at least was the theory, but enemy bombardments might easily sever the communication wires.

It was against this background that Beppe would have his first taste of battle.

CHAPTER III

The Battle for Monte Grappa

The main summits of Monte Grappa are about three kilometres west of the edge of the Piave plain which runs from Bassano to Pederobba, a distance of around fifteen kilometres. The lower slopes consist of woods and the upper slopes are generally open and grassy in summer. On the west side Grappa is separated from the Asiago plateau by the Brenta Valley. In good weather there is an extensive view from the top of Monte Grappa, the summit of which is at 1,775 metres. From the summit long ridges extend north for ten kilometres to end at Monte Roncone and Monte Tomatico.

Monte Grappa represented a strategic position linking the Asiago and Piave fronts and dominated the surrounding country in all directions. It was for this reason that General Cadorna in 1916 ordered the building of a road from Bassano in the south to the southern end of Monte Grappa. By now, in late 1917, this included two supply cableways and further extensive fortifications on the mountain.

Beppe and 3rd Alpini Regiment were now dug into defensive positions on Monte Tomba. From the great ridge of the mountain, which is to the northeast on Monte Grappa, the Piave river and its trenches were in full sight of the enemy. If Monte Tomba was taken by the Austrians, their forward observers on the top of the mountain could direct artillery in support of Austrian river crossings, or help defeat Italian counterattacks.

The first battle of Monte Grappa started on 11 November 1917.

The Austrians had asked for German help and the German high command sent seven battle-tried divisions. One of the German battalions was the Württemberg Mountain Battalion, in which First Lieutenant Erwin Rommel was a young detachment commander of three mountain companies and a machine-gun company. Rommel had previously been fighting in Romania, and in October 1917 his battalion, part of the newly created Fourteenth Army attached to the German Alpenkorps, was deployed to the Italian front.

In 1937 Rommel was to publish *Infantry Attacks*. He intended it to be an infantry textbook based on his experiences in World War I. When he wrote the book he was the commander of a Jäger-Bataillon in the Harz Mountains.

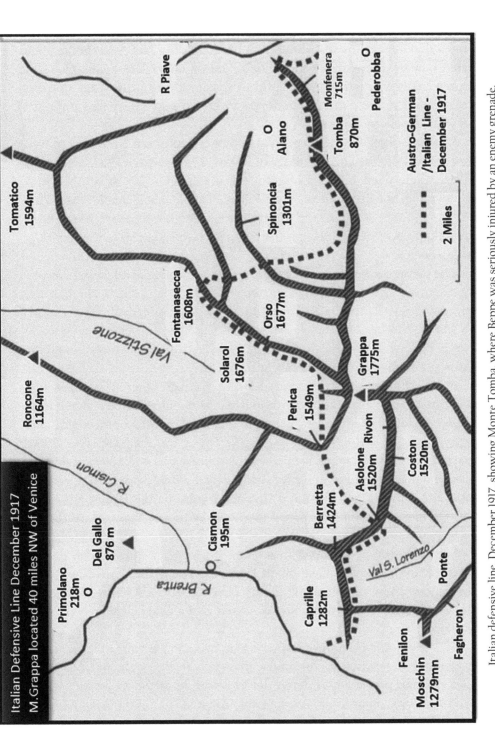

Italian defensive line, December 1917, showing Monte Tomba, where Beppe was seriously injured by an enemy grenade.

Italian Defensive Line December 1917
M.Grappa located 40 miles NW of Venice

Tomatico 1594m

R Piave

Monfenera 715m

Pederobba

O Alano

Spinoncia 1301m

Tomba 870m

Austro-German /Italian Line – December 1917

2 Miles

Fontanasecca 1608m

Val Stizzone

Orso 1677m

Solarol 1676m

Roncone 1164m

Perica 1549m

Grappa 1775m

R Cismon

Del Gallo 876 m

Asolone Rivon 1520m

Coston 1520m

Berretta 1424m

Cismon 195m

Primolano 218m

R Brenta

Val S. Lorenzo

Ponte

Caprille 1282m

Fenilon

Moschin 1279mn

Fagheron

In a touch of irony this battalion, during the Napoleonic Wars, fought for England in the capture of Gibraltar. In his book, Rommel describes in great detail how the German soldiers fought and the lessons to be learnt.[7] This source has been particularly helpful to the author, as it provides valuable background to the battles that Beppe fought in and which had not been previously well documented.

Rommel describes how the Württemberg Mountain Battalion moved into the second line and had a day of rest on 11 November 1917, when they buried their dead in the Longarone cemetery. On 17 November they deployed to the River Piave from Feltre. A fierce engagement was taking place in the area of Quero and Monte Tomba, and the Germans found great difficulty in advancing through the narrow Piave valley, which was packed with troops.

The Germans were soon within range of the Italian artillery, which was bombarding the valley road. Rommel had been informed that the advancing Austrian units had encountered well-defended enemy positions on Monte Tomba. The Italian artillery had excellent observation posts on Monte Pallone and Monte Tomba and was able to direct accurate fire on the defile at Quero and on all key mounting areas.

At last light the Germans moved swiftly through Quero. The town had been badly damaged and continued to be bombarded by the Italian artillery. Craters of up to ten metres in diameter hindered movement, and many dead and wounded German Jägers lay by the roadside. The Italian searchlights turned night into day and illuminated the valley from the direction of Monte Tomba. Heavy shelling by the Italians gave the Germans only brief moments to continue advancing towards the Italian positions. The Germans were being exposed to a combination of shrapnel, rocks and earth raining down on them.

Rommel soon appreciated that it was no longer a question of a quick advance across Monte Grappa to Bassano. The Italian positions were continuous and well defended, and he realised that the Germans were too late. Six French and five English divisions had already deployed into the front to shore up the Italian forces.

This first battle of Monte Grappa was to become the most well known, as it brought the Austrian summer offensive of 1917 to a halt. General Cadorna had previously ordered the fortification of the mountain, which had effectively made it an impregnable fortress. The Austrians, with the

---

[7] Erwin Rommel, *Infantry Attacks* (Barnsley: Frontline, 2019)

help of the German army's Alpenkorps, had failed to take the mountain. This decisive victory saved Italy by stabilising the Italian front along the Piave river.

On 12 November the Austro-German army had advanced southwards along the spurs leading up to Monte Grappa. The Italian forward defences on Monte Roncone and Monte Tomatico held, but on 18 November the Austro-German army launched an attack on the main Italian defensive positions. The northern edge of the Grappa massif became the front line. By nightfall it became clear that the attack had failed. The Austrians had been unable to bring their artillery far enough forward to support their attacks, and lacked essential supplies and munitions. There had been no element of surprise for the Italians, who had their best troops defending the Monte Grappa positions.

The Italians were also encouraged by the deployment of British, US, French and British empire troops which had started in November. They were now confident that they could hold the line of the Piave and Monte Grappa.

On 19 November Beppe's battalion attacked the tactically important high ground of Monte Nero. The attack was successful and the Battalion was later to be awarded the Silver Medal of Valour for this victory. Casualties were high and included Beppe who was shot in the thigh. He was very fortunate to survive. His left leg was shattered and he lost a lot of blood. He was evacuated to the rear of the Italian defensive position and eventually to an ambulance, which took him to a military hospital in Carrara, Tuscany. It was unlikely that there would have been sufficient supplies of morphine to relieve the pain during the journey. His condition was critical and the army surgeons at the military hospital decided that amputation of his left leg was the only solution.

Beppe fully appreciated the seriousness of his condition. He had decided against living with only one leg and asked the surgeon to leave his pistol by the bedside if his leg was to be amputated.

His father, however, on hearing of

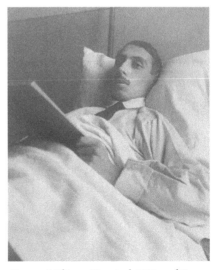

Carrera Military Hospital, 1917, and Beppe recovering from his operations.

the seriousness of his son's condition, assembled a team of highly experienced surgeons from Turin. This team travelled to Carrara, took over
medical responsibility for the young Beppe and made their assessment.
They decided that his left leg could be saved, and indeed it was, but it took
fourteen separate operations.

The Italians continued to fight fiercely in Beppe's absence. Many peaks
changed hands, but on 28 December 1917 Monte Asolone and Col della
Beretta were recaptured from the Austro-German side by the Abruzzi
Brigade and the Alpini, with whom Beppe had served. On 30 December,
supported by British artillery, the French recaptured Monte Tomba, ending
combat on Monte Grappa.

In early January 1918, Rommel was reassigned to a higher headquarters
as a staff officer. He much regretted not being able to rejoin the
Württemberg Mountain Battalion, but he followed its progress during the
last year of the war, which included several battles on the Western Front.
Rommel ends his book by acknowledging the deaths of many of his soldiers,
which he describes as a constant reminder to those who survived that they
must not fail when it becomes a question of making sacrifices for Germany.

Rommel was awarded the Pour le Merite for his actions on the Italian
Front, the highest Prussian order for valour. Rommel was to go on to be one
of the most highly respected commanders in World War II. Sadly, in 1944,
whilst recovering from his injuries after his staff car was hit by a British
fighter aircraft in Normandy, he was implicated in the 20 July plot to
assassinate Hitler. Rommel was a national hero, and so Hitler decided that
Rommel should be eliminated quietly. Rommel was given the choice of
death by suicide or facing a trial which would have ended with his execution
and the persecution of his family. He chose suicide and was given a state
funeral following the announcement that he had died of his wounds.

*

Although the Austrians could see Venice, they would never reach it. The
battle along the Piave river, the main effort of the Austrian attack, was a
disaster. Despite being outnumbered two to one, the Italian line held.
Intercepted radio messages revealed the coming attack, and Italian artillery
pounded the Austro-Hungarian assembly areas. Then, on 17 June 1918, a
bridgehead across the Piave seven kilometres deep and twenty wide was lost
as the river flooded due to heavy rains in the mountains. In this area alone
24,000 Austrians were cut off from retreat and captured. The storms that

had led to the initial Austro-Hungarian success on Monte Grappa now resulted in the catastrophe on the flood plains below. Italian and Canadian aircraft were able to destroy enemy pontoon bridges attempting a rescue.

The Great War Society history of the war records that a young American Red Cross volunteer, Ernest Hemingway, also witnessed the battles on Monte Grappa and the Piave. He had been wounded while carrying rations to Italian troops, and he wrote home about the ferocity of the battle and the many dead Austrians. He was also in awe of the bravery of the Italian soldiers, and Hemingway was later to write his autobiographical novel, *A Farewell to Arms*, based on his experiences.

After hearing of Austria's disaster, the German foreign secretary told his government not to expect an end to the war by military means alone. The Germans had placed great hope in this offensive. Victory in the Alps might result in better peace terms with the Allies, something which was being seriously considered in Berlin and Vienna.

Austrian losses were close to 180,000, including over 35,000 on Monte Grappa. Italian casualties totalled nearly 85,000, with 14,000 on the mountain. The single French and the two British divisions that participated on the Piave front suffered over 3,000 killed, missing or wounded.

The French Allied commander General Foch urged the Italian commander General Diaz to exploit the victory with a counteroffensive. Diaz refused, replying that an Italian counterattack would be as costly as the casualties that the Austrians had just suffered.

Italy had survived one of the greatest offensives of the war and now held the line during a second onslaught, both battles having the Grappa massif as the objective. The mighty peak where Beppe had been very seriously injured would now witness Italy's greatest victory. In a hostile alpine environment, with few resources and little support from their government, Italy's army gave an impressive performance and prevailed at Monte Grappa.

History has rightly not looked favourably on Cadorna. Arrogant, stubborn and somewhat deluded, he imagined himself as a successor to Napoleon. His reaction to defeats was to sack his commanders, and it is said that he even followed the Roman tactic of executing every tenth man (decimation) in any unit that had failed to perform in battle. This is unlikely, but during the course of the war he dismissed 217 officers, and during the Battle of Caporetto he ordered the summary execution of officers whose units retreated. Despite the disaster of Caporetto, Cadorna held on to his position, mainly due to his support from the king.

Italian war memorial at Monte Grappa. Completed in 1935, it contains the graves of 22,950 Italian soldiers, although the mountain originally had 140 small cemeteries with the remains of around 40,000 dead.

The arrival of the British and French led to Cadorna's replacement, as they rightly insisted on his removal. Cadorna was replaced by General Diaz, who was a significant improvement and avoided costly offensives until the time was right. In October 1918 he ordered the offensive which became known as the Battle of Vittorio Veneto. With the support of British and French units, Italy won the day and the Austrian-Hungarian empire was effectively destroyed.

Italy had suffered over one million casualties over the course of the war, of which two thirds were killed: this from a population of only 35 million. The reluctance of many Italians to fight later in Ethiopia and in World War II may have its origins in the appalling family losses in World War I.

During much of this time Beppe was still in Carrara military hospital, recovering from his operations. Postcards from his siblings wishing him well in his recovery, dated March 1918, indicate that he spent at least four months in hospital.

Miraculously, and with the skills of his father's surgeons, Beppe's leg was saved. There was a serious implication, however, as Beppe was left unable to walk. Slowly, and with continued treatment and exercise, he learnt to walk again, but only with the use of a stick. For a young man in the prime of his life, and with a love of sport and the outdoor life, this must have been a devastating blow. He never complained, but life from now on would be very different.

His father, appreciating Beppe's life-changing disability, asked his son what he would like to do with his life. Beppe immediately replied that he wanted to paint, and with his father's means and resources this would now be possible.

The horrors of war and his own suffering may have had an indelible effect on Beppe's mind, and may explain the grotesque but accurate depictions of war in his paintings.

CHAPTER IV

Return to Turin and Marriage

Beppe returned to Turin to recuperate after his operations. Always elegantly dressed, he must have cut a fine figure in Turin society. He was a popular young man with a wide circle of friends amongst the well-educated and privileged Turin families.

Although his art was clearly central to his life, Beppe still had time to observe an attractive young lady who walked to work each day past the Porcheddu garden in Turin. Beppe discovered that the girl worked in a millinery shop. Over the next few months he was to find various excuses to buy items for his sisters from the shop.

The young lady was Margherita Pasqua Bussolino. She was born on 17 April 1897 in Moncalieri, the daughter of Battista and Lanfranco Maria Bussolino. The two families probably had little in common, but Margherita was both beautiful and charming, and Beppe's father was delighted when his son introduced her to the family. Marriage followed on 11 July 1924 at Villafranca d'Asti, thirty kilometres southeast of Turin. Their twin daughters, Giovanna and Amalia (Ninilla), were born on 3 November 1925, and a son, Giovanni Battista (Bitita), two years later on 6 January 1927.

Beppe Porcheddu in 1922 with a permanent disability, needing a walking stick as a result of his World War I injuries. Ross Family Archive.

Rita, as Margherita became known to everyone, was the centre of the family and, whilst Beppe involved himself in his painting, Rita ran the home and the finances. This was probably just as well, as Beppe seemed uninterested in the accumulation of wealth at all, let alone the day-to-day business of petty cash and household budgets. Perhaps it was because he had never had to worry about money throughout his early years. Even after Beppe married and had children, he and his adult siblings received a weekly allowance from their father. All the extended family were able to live in Giovanni's large villa in the centre of Turin, which had over forty rooms, and the weekly ritual of the allowance handout became embedded. It was therefore unsurprising that money was never an incentive for Beppe or his siblings.

Beppe had been invalided out of the army and awarded a full war pension in the highest category. Although he was fortunate not to require such a pension in the early years of marriage, it was to become an important source of income during the more difficult times of World War II and later for Rita.

In the Turin villa, the grandchildren occupied the nursery wing at the top of the house but were allowed to go and say goodnight to their

Margherita (Rita) with her children: the author's mother and her twin sister. Turin, 1929.

parents and grandfather when the family were assembled for dinner. Tragically, Giovanni's young wife, Amalia, had died during childbirth in 1912.

The villa had extensive grounds, despite being in the centre of Turin. There were glasshouses providing much of the vegetables, a huge aviary stocked with a large collection of indigenous and exotic birds, and several dogs, which mostly lived in kennels during the day but roamed around the grounds at night. There was even a donkey, which would be attached to a trap to transport the children around the grounds and Turin.

The garage had a number of cars, a rarity in Italy in those years and a mark of significant affluence. The children would sometimes go and play inside the cars, and the smell of the green leather seats in one of them became a childhood memory for the young grandchildren. Another shared childhood memory was a park in Turin where one day Beppe and his family saw a child's electric car being tried out by its inventor. Beppe immediately asked if he could buy it, and so the twins had their first car.

In Turin the Porcheddus' wide circle of family friends included the Agnellis (who founded Fiat), the Cinzanos and the Olivettis. Giovanni Porcheddu, recognising the potential of Camillo Olivetti and his typing machine, lent him money to expand his business.

These families were also instrumental in the rise of Juventus as one of the most successful Italian football teams. They supported the team financially, and the home games became important social occasions for all the families. Edoardo Agnelli gained control of the club in 1923 and a new stadium was built.

Life in Turin after the war was very pleasant for the Porcheddu family. Beppe's father had designed and constructed another family villa in Cavoretto, a very old district on the outskirts of Turin. Beppe and his family often stayed there as a change from the centre of Turin, although Alassio on the Ligurian coast became their favourite for the summer months. The family also often lived in Nice for the winter, with a family tutor in tow so that schooling was never neglected.

Beppe, who had trained as an architect, designed and arranged the building of a large family villa in Merano, a city in South Tyrol famous for its spas. After World War I the city was annexed to Italy from Austria-Hungary, along with much of South Tyrol. Many of Beppe's original design drawings for the villa still remain in the family archive.

The family spent a considerable amount of time in Merano: so much so that Beppe's children attended the local school, where all the lessons were conducted entirely in German. Indeed, the working language of Merano was German, as it bordered the German-speaking area of Austria. At home Beppe insisted that the whole family speak French. Languages were to become a particular strength of Beppe's children.

The children often skied to school, and these were particularly happy times for the Porcheddu family. Beppe, however, could be a hard taskmaster when it came to school and music lessons.

Often melancholy, Beppe nevertheless retained a sense of humour. Rita's optimism and practicality must have been a great foil to him. Beppe even encouraged Rita to learn French and to play the piano. Rita had not had Beppe's privileged upbringing and education, so perhaps this was something of a Pygmalion tendency he had.

All in all, life was pretty glamorous for the family and Rita was able to dress more elegantly than she had ever imagined as a young working girl in Turin. She made trips to Paris, accompanied by her sister-in-law, Elsa, to visit the fashion house of Madame Jeanne-Marie Lanvin (1867–1944). They would return with new wardrobes. On other occasions both Beppe and Rita would visit Paris for several months at a time, enjoying the café society and the company of other artists and intellectuals. Their children were left behind in Turin with governesses.

CHAPTER V

The Rise of Mussolini

In the post-war period, Beppe was quick to identify the dangers of Benito Mussolini (1883–1945) and the politics of his fascist party.

Before World War I Mussolini had been the editor of *Il Popolo d'Italia*, which was subsidised by countries eager for Italy to join the side of the Allies. He had joined the army during the war but was discharged in 1917 as a result of injuries sustained in the accidental explosion of a mortar bomb in his trench. He left, however, with the reputation of having been a brave and capable soldier. It is believed that his lavish lifestyle in post-war Milan was largely funded by the British Secret Service, as the British government believed that support for Mussolini would keep the communists from power.

Benito Mussolini, badly wounded in World War I and now a fascist dictator.

In 1919 Mussolini formed a movement called the Fasci di Combattimento ('the fighting group'), bringing together a number of disparate groups united by their general disenchantment with the socialism of post-war Italy. This movement was to become the fascist party. At first it had little support, but, as concern grew in Italy in the direction of the socialists and with the rise of communism, more Italians turned towards Mussolini. Realising the importance of Garibaldi to many Italians in the reunification of Italy, Mussolini claimed that his Blackshirts were the descendants of Garibaldi and his Redshirts.

An important factor in fascism gaining support in its early days was because it opposed discrimination and any sort of division based on social class. Little did its supporters know that it would lead to an effective dictatorship. Mussolini probably even inspired Adolf Hitler.

Fascism led to many family arguments between Beppe and his father. Beppe's father supported Mussolini, but only for his social policies. Giovanni, probably as a result of his own very difficult and impoverished childhood, was a firm supporter of Mussolini's efforts to reduce poverty and to help the less fortunate.

Italy's pension system owes itself to one of Mussolini's initiatives. Under him there was an expansion of building roads, bridges and sporting facilities, as well as a number of dramatic buildings and memorials in Rome, as if challenging the ancient Romans and their architecture. Even today, many Italians continue to have a secret admiration for Mussolini, and often not so secret. Despite his despotic regime and the murder and imprisonment of those who opposed him, his achievements continue to be recognised. Under him Italy was modernised, but it is clear that a few Italians have forgotten or ignored his assassination of political rivals, his persecution of the Jews, his ill-judged excursion into Abyssinia and his alliance with Hitler.

A report in the *Guardian* by Angela Giuffrida, published on 27 July 2019, describes the visit of supporters of Mussolini to Predappio, the birth town and burial place of Mussolini. As many as 100,000 people, it has been estimated, visit the town each year. Many of these may merely be curious tourists, but thousands are fascist pilgrims, who parade to Mussolini's tomb on occasions such as the anniversary of his birth and death.

The town's right-wing mayor, Roberto Canali, announced in 2019 that the crypt would now be open all year round, having previously been closed to the public for most of the year. Italy's anti-fascist association ANPI, in a statement, said, 'This muddies the memories of many of the victims of fascist crime, its racial laws and collaboration with the Nazis that led to the massacre of innocent women, men and children.'[8]

It is clear that support for fascism still exists within the far right in Italian politics. Beppe would have been much saddened and disappointed by such support.

Another part of Giovanni's wider family also supported fascism. One of his children, Ambrogia (born in Turin on 25 July 1899), was married in 1926 to Giorgio Bardanzellu, a famous Sardinian lawyer who now lived in Turin. They had three children. Giorgio served with distinction in the Italian infantry and was decorated for bravery, and was then wounded in

---

[8] Angela Giuffrida, 'Mussolini's birthplace cashes in on the surge of far-right tourism', *The Guardian*, 27 July 2019

Motherhood by Beppe, 1928, pastels on coloured paper.

the Battle of Monte Grappa fighting against the Austrians. After the war he continued a distinguished legal career and was knighted in 1931. He entered politics, becoming a deputy (member of the Italian parliament) in the fascist party in 1932. This caused a major family rift with Beppe, who would not entertain any pro-fascist sentiments.

After the war Bardanzellu continued in politics and became a deputy in the monarchist party, serving two terms in 1953 and 1958. One of his key acts was to bring in a highway code and speed limits for Italian roads: probably a significant achievement! He died in 1974.

Beppe, like his father, supported social reform, but Beppe was adamantly against any dictatorship, no matter how seemingly benign. He was of a different generation to his father. He had experienced the ravages of war; he predicted the disastrous path that Italy was embarking on under the rise of Mussolini. He was an artist with no need to compromise his views, unlike his father, who would have had to work with the fascist regime in order to bid for the many building contracts that were being awarded during the dictatorship of Mussolini.

In October 1922 Mussolini's fascist Blackshirts gathered in Rome to demand the resignation of the liberal prime minister, Luigi Facta. The Milizia Volontaria per la Sicurezza Nazionale, commonly called the Blackshirts, had been

The Jungle by Beppe, pen and ink.

Joan of Arc by Beppe, 1929, ceramic manufactured by Lenci.

established in 1919. Many were former soldiers, and they were able to gather support in their opposition to the rise of the socialists. The king refused the government's request to impose martial law and handed over power to Mussolini, inviting him to form a government. The king and the conservative establishment had feared civil war and thought Mussolini would be able to restore order, but they failed to foresee the dangers ahead.

On becoming the youngest prime minister in Italy's history in 1922, Mussolini made it clear that he despised democracy. Gradually he increased his powers, and by 1929 he held the majority of cabinet posts himself. Those who opposed him were sidelined or even murdered, and soon all political parties, except Mussolini's Partito Nazionale Fascista, had been banned. Beppe was vocal in his opposition and would publicly call the strutting Mussolini 'Pagliaccio' ('the clown').

Despite his anti-fascism, Beppe was becoming well known as an illustrator of children's stories. His first illustrations had appeared as early as 1919 in the magazine *The Pasquino* and then in many other periodicals, including the *Corriere dei Piccoli* and *Mickey Mouse*. He joined the artistic section of

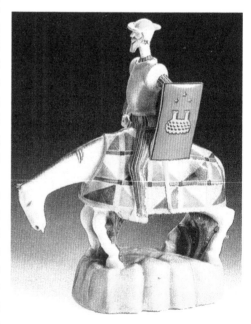

Don Quixote by Beppe, 1929, ceramic manufactured by Lenci.

Beppe's Certificate of Knighthood, 18 January 1925. Beppe was knighted by King Victor Emmanuel III for his contribution to the arts.

Edizioni De Agostini, for which he created the major designs and illustrations of the *Great Prose Writers* series and for the novel *Angel of Kindness* by Ippolito Nievo.

Beppe turned his artistic talent to the design of dolls, toys and ceramics. Between 1920 and 1929 he was the artistic director of the De Agostini publications and was responsible for a string of literary articles.

In recognition of his major contribution to the arts, Beppe was knighted by King Victor Emmanuel III on 28 January 1925.[9] He therefore followed his father, who had also been knighted for services to the construction industry. Beppe was only twenty-seven when he was knighted, and many of his greatest works were still to be painted.

In 1926 Arnaldo Cipolla's *Il cuore dei continenti* ('The Heart of the Continents') was illustrated by Beppe and published by Mondadori. Cipolla was one of Italy's foremost journalists, explorers and writers. After army service in the Congo in 1904 he became a war correspondent, covering Italian actions in Somalia, Ethiopia and Libya. He drew on his experiences to write a number of very successful novels, of which *Il cuore dei continenti* was one. Beppe's distinctive style perfectly complemented Cipolla's descriptive writing.

The Supper at Emmaus by Beppe, 1936, watercolour on maple. Galleria D'Arte Narciso, Turin.

---

[9] Certificate of Knighthood Number 123023, 28 January 1925 (Ross Archive)

Beppe exhibited all over Italy and in 1929 participated in a major presentation by Lenci at the Pesaro gallery in Milan. The company, based in Turin, became world-famous for its ceramics and pressed woollen felt dolls. In 1937 the firm employed 300 workers. Beppe's drawings became the models for many ceramic pieces, now much sought after. The Lenci factory was bombed by the Allies in 1944.

Pre-war Italy became a difficult and dangerous place for anyone who opposed fascism and Mussolini. Beppe was a close friend of Carlo Levi. Levi, also from Turin, was a doctor by training but

The Saint by Beppe, 1936, watercolour on maple.
Galleria D'Arte Narciso, Turin.

an artist by profession. Like Beppe, he was an anti-fascist. In 1935 Levi was sentenced to internal exile for his views and sent to a village in the hills of Basilicata. He was sympathetic to the poverty suffered by the Italians in the south, unlike many northerners. Ten years later he was to write *Christ Stopped at Eboli*. The book was based on his experiences, incorporated into a fictional tale of impoverished villagers oppressed by the regulations of the regime they were under.

In 1935 Mussolini invaded Abyssinia, not only to strengthen Italy's position in Africa alongside its existing colonies of Tigre and Somaliland, but also to avenge the defeat of the Italian army at the Battle of Adwa in 1896. Now victory was secured in just six months. There followed support for General Franco in the Spanish Civil War, which resulted in depleting Italian military resources in the run-up to the country's entry into World War II.

By the late 1930s, Mussolini had concluded that Britain and France were in decline and that it would be Germany and Italy who would dominate Europe. This led naturally to an alliance with Germany following Italy's invasion of Albania in 1939.

Beppe's anti-fascist views were becoming well known in Turin, and he decided to act before the inevitable consequences. He decided to join a close Italian friend of his, Professor Raffaello Monti, also an anti-fascist, who had moved temporarily to Toulouse with his family in the mid-1930s to escape the now toxic atmosphere in Italy.

In 1936 Beppe and the whole family moved to Toulouse to live with Monti and his family. They were to stay there for a year, and the children attended French schools. In fact, Beppe insisted that French be spoken at home and his letters to his children were often in French. Even so, my mother always commented that Beppe was very much an Anglophile, perhaps as a result of his interest in the great British illustrators or the reputation the United Kingdom had for democracy and freedom of speech.

Beppe's family priorities of education, music and the arts continued under his somewhat strict direction. He would timetable academic and musical studies for the children. Life was therefore carefully structured and the upbringing of his children probably very different to the other young people they met and befriended. Rita's optimism and practicality must have been a great foil to Beppe's often stern demeanour, although he did not lack a sense of humour.

Both families, however, were forced to return to Italy, as it was becoming impossible to transfer funds from Italy to France. On re-entry to Italy, Beppe had his passport temporarily withdrawn, such was his anti-fascist reputation.

The Porcheddu family returned to Turin and then for a short period to the family villa in Merano. For the family these continued to be particularly happy times, as my mother would describe. Rita, no doubt at home in the country, kept a number of animals, including a goat, and enjoyed bottling fruit in huge glass jars for the winter. She was an excellent cook and family meals together were much enjoyed. The children still skied to school, and the family also had a German governess who gave them skiing lessons and showed them how to make a piste in the morning on new snow. Beppe's abhorrence, however, for fascist politics was to shape his future direction and actions as the rise of Nazism and fascism cast their dark shadows over Europe.

In 1933, Beppe illustrated a book entitled *Il fanciullo che vola* ('The Child Who Flies'). It was published under the pseudonym Diaroma, and the author's name is not known. It contains a dedication by Italo Balbo: 'I believe that this operetta [sic], inspired by the life of aviators and written with grace, will help spread the passion for flying among the very new generations.'

The involvement of Balbo is interesting. Italo Balbo (1896–1940) was an

Rita and the Porcheddu children with their favourite donkey and trap.

Italian fascist leader, a marshal of the air force and commander-in-chief of Italian North Africa in World War II. He was the only leading fascist to oppose Mussolini's alliance with Hitler. In World War I, like Beppe, he had fought the Austrians and Germans as an Alpini officer. He was decorated for bravery. After the war he entered politics as a fascist and subsequently was instrumental in building up the Italian air force. Ironically, in 1940 he was mistakenly shot down in Libya by an Italian anti-aircraft battery. Such was his reputation as an honourable soldier and aviator that the British dropped a wreath over the airfield with a note of condolences.

It is interesting to speculate on why Beppe, a fervent anti-fascist, would become involved in a publication supported by Balbo. Perhaps it was just a commercial matter. On the other hand, Balbo had been a fellow Alpini officer.

In 1938 Beppe was to design the set of the film adaptation of *Ettore Fieramosca*, a book written by one of Italy's most colourful characters, Massimo d'Azeglio, who had been prime minister of Piedmont in 1849 at the age of fifty. The director of the film was Alessandro Blasetti, who has been credited as the driving force in the revival of the Italian film industry in the 1930s. Fieramosca was an Italian nobleman, born in 1476, who fought in various European wars. He was adopted as something of a national legend and hero during the Risorgimento and then during the rise of fascism. Beppe was to comment that he thought the film did indeed have fascist undertones, but he enjoyed the challenge of being a film set designer, for which he was to be widely acclaimed. Beppe's daughter Giovanna recalls her entire school in Turin attending a showing of the film,[10] no doubt a welcome relief from lessons.

The impending second great war of the twentieth century forced Beppe to make another key change to family life.

---

[10] Interview, author and Giovanna Ross (née Porcheddu), 2016

CHAPTER VI

The Move to Bordighera

In early 1941 Beppe and his family left Merano and moved to Bordighera, a picturesque town on the Ligurian coast. The town is situated not far from the border town of Ventimiglia with its Roman theatre, a well-preserved 5,000-seater from the second century. On the coast near the French border is where one of Europe's most advanced Palaeolithic cultures lived in cliffside caves at Balzi Rossi ('red cliffs'): first Neanderthals (80,000–35,000 years ago) and later Homo sapiens (35,000–10,000 years ago). The drawing of a horse on a cave wall is a particular attraction, as are various artefacts from the era exhibited in the museum on the site. Sadly, much of the collection was destroyed during the Second World War when the rail tunnels were blown up.

Bordighera was indirectly connected to Beppe through his war days on the Italian front. The Italian commander had been General Cadorna and, after his retirement, he had moved to Bordighera, where he died in 1928. Cadorna's son Raffaele became a general in the Second World War and, after the armistice, joined the partisans and fought against the Germans.

Bordighera, Liguria, on the Italian Riviera. Located twenty kilometres from France, seen in the background.

Beppe had become increasingly pessimistic as to the outcome for Italy following the start of World War II. He ominously predicted that Italy would eventually enter the war on the side of Germany. It did so on 10 June 1940, when France was about to fall and World War II seemed about to end.

As with Italy's entry into World War I, then on the side of the Allies, the aim was to achieve territorial gains on the country's northern border with Austria. When Mussolini decided to side with Germany, one of his reasons was that Italy had felt let down after World War I by the Allies, who had reneged on territorial promises they had made in order to entice Italy to enter the war on their side.

Mussolini's decision was opposed by his foreign minister, Galeazzo Ciano, but to no avail, despite Ciano being Mussolini's son-in law. Ciano was later to be shot, after being tried by a fascist court, for voting out Mussolini in July 1943.

As Beppe's home town of Turin was at the centre of a very important industrial area, he suspected it was likely to be an attractive target for Allied bombing. He was to be proved correct, and therefore Bordighera, a place of relative unimportance in terms of Italy's war effort, was a much safer place for the young Porcheddu family. An added advantage was that Beppe's elder brother Mario, along with his family, had already moved to Bordighera. Mario, who had trained as a lawyer, was now the director of the San Remo Casino. Although its origins were in games and gambling, the casino was now much more a cultural centre for the region. Beppe's old friend from Turin and Toulouse, Professore Monti, also now lived in Bordighera.

Mario, like all the Porcheddu family, was very well connected. He was able to encourage famous opera singers, classical dancers, ballet companies, actors, musicians and orchestras to come to San Remo and to perform at the casino for the affluent Italians and the many foreigners who lived there. It was described as the golden period of the casino, largely as a result of the work of Mario. Mario, however, understood that, for him and the casino to succeed in fascist Italy, compromise and accommodation were the necessities of life. Mario's acceptance of Mussolini and fascism was to lead to numerous arguments with Beppe.

Mario's only son, Gian Antonio,[11] was himself to become a well-known artist in Italy. He was born in Bordighera on 4 January 1920. Like his uncle,

---

[11] Angelo Dragone, *Gian Antonio* (Ventimiglia: Tipolitografia, 1979)

Beppe, he was largely self-taught and had been drawing and painting since an early age. He graduated from the University of Turin in law in 1942 and in political and social sciences in 1947. His only ambition, however, was to be a painter.

Antonio exhibited throughout Europe, his most important personal exhibitions being at the Ciliberti Gallery in 1945 and in 1947 at the Borgonuovo Gallery, both in Milan. In 1955 he exhibited at La Fondation d'Art de la Napoule. Later, in 1957, he exhibited in the United States. In 1958 he was invited by Lionello Venturi, of the Rome–New York Art Foundation, to exhibit in the 'New Trends in Italian Art'. He also exhibited in Genoa and Mainz for the Vereinigung Bildender Künstler und V. Zentrum Mainz. He was the only Italian artist invited to exhibit in the Kunstausstellung Donaueschingen of 1960.

Between 1960 and 1969 he took part in various important exhibitions in Italy and abroad. In April 1963 he exhibited in Milan in the Palazzo della Permanente, in 1970 in Venice and Monte Carlo. His final exhibition took place in Bordighera at the Grand Hotel del Mare in the summer of 1972. He died tragically on 10 January 1973 from blood poisoning following a suicide attempt.

Works by Gian Antonio appear in many of the most important private collections in Italy and elsewhere. Amongst those who acclaimed his talent was Peggy Guggenheim in 1948 in Venice, where he was taking part in the Venice Biennale, the most important platform for European contemporary art. Guggenheim implored him to go to New York with her to take his place amongst the American abstract expressionists. But, despite her offers of fame in the States, he preferred to tread his own path and remained in Italy. Others who have written about him include Germano Beringheli, Marziano Bernardi, Leonardo Borgese, Massimo Cavalli, Cesare Chirici, Vincenzo Costantini, Donatella D'Imporzano, Angelo Dragone, Albino Galvano, Marco Valsecchi and Lionello Venturi.

Mario's wife, Elsa, from a Jewish German family of Turin, was related to Guido Hess, who also lived in Bordighera. Guido Hess (1909–1990) was a well-known Italian journalist, poet, painter and writer. He was yet another notable anti-fascist who had joined the partisans and who became a socialist after the war. A talented and charismatic man, he was typical of the free-thinking and liberal-minded young professionals and artists who lived in the Bordighera area in post-war Italy such as Italo Calvino, Giuseppe Balbo and Salvatore Quasimodo. Peggy Guggenheim visited Bordighera for an exhibition of American artists organised by Balbo. Quasimodo was to win the Nobel Prize for Literature in 1959, the year after Boris Pasternak was honoured.

This new generation of Italian artists, writers and poets were largely anti-establishment yet tolerant. They had felt deeply let down by the chaos in Europe, the wars that Italy had been led into, the malign reign of Mussolini and Italian efforts to recreate an empire, such as the tragic excursion into Abyssinia in October 1935. There was a better way, they thought, and immersing themselves in the arts may have been a way of isolating themselves from the corrupt and negative politics of the day. Bordighera was also a magnet to many famous visitors in the nineteenth and twentieth centuries attracted by its climate, history, architecture and culture.

The Porcheddu family's first home in Bordighera was in Via dei Colli, where No. 41 occupied a commanding view over the town. Bordighera not only had a thriving artistic community at the time but had long been a magnet for artists and writers attracted by the climate, architecture and vistas.

Claude Monet in Bordighera Old Town during one of his visits, 1883.

One such famous artist in the previous century was Claude Monet.

Monet first visited Bordighera with his friend Pierre-Auguste Renoir in 1883. He visited more as a tourist than an artist, but he was to return again by himself in 1884. On 12 January 1884 he wrote to Paul Durand-Ruel, the Parisian art dealer, who did much to support and fund the Impressionists and to promote their works to the United States market. In his letter Monet tells Durand-Ruel that he has decided to spend a month in Bordighera. In fact he stayed until April. He describes Bordighera as one of the most beautiful places he has seen, but he also says that this trip must remain a secret. Much as he enjoyed visiting the town the previous year with Renoir, he needed to be alone if he was to paint.

This period was one of Monet's most prolific, often working on six

Bordighera by Claude Monet. SPADEM, Paris

canvasses a day and at times finishing one a day. Many of his most famous landscapes were painted in Bordighera and along the French Riviera. Bordighera, with its palm trees, its citrus groves and its micro-climate of warm, sunny summers and mild winters, was a revelation to Monet. Monet had discovered the power of colour, which is clearly evident in his canvasses from this period. In a letter to the sculptor Auguste Rodin describing his efforts to translate into paint the brilliant Mediterranean light, Monet said he was 'fencing, wrestling, with the sun'.[12] Monet's *Bordighera* was painted from a tower built on a prominent hill overlooking Bordighera. The watchtower, named Torre dei Mostaccini, was built in the fifteenth century in order to give early warning of the arrival of Turkish pirates.

Monet had been inspired by the colour and beauty of the Ligurian coast and the abundance of flowers as well as the architecture and well-preserved buildings, many of which dated back to the eleventh century. Monet was

---

[12] Letter, Monet to Auguste Rodin, 1884 (Art Institute of Chicago Catalogue)

aged forty-four at the time he was in Bordighera and was yet to achieve acclaim as an artist. His use of colour in his paintings in Bordighera is most striking and very different to his later years during his so called 'Blue Period', when Monet's failing eyesight, as a result of cataracts, affected his work. His canvases then were mainly in blue, which is possibly because it was the only colour he could see.

Up until his visits to Bordighera, Monet's paintings generally did not command high prices, but there occurred a dramatic change in his fortunes following US interest in his paintings of Bordighera and the south of France. He quickly became very much in demand as an artist. As a result of the much higher value of his paintings, Monet was able to buy a house at Giverny, which his family had been renting for some years, and to live very comfortably in comparison to his earlier years as an artist.

Bordighera was also the venue for a meeting between Mussolini and the Spanish dictator General Francisco Franco on 11 February 1941. They met in Villa Margherita, the Riviera home of the Queen. Mussolini wanted to discuss with Franco whether Spain would enter the war on the side of Germany and Italy. The entry of Spain on the side of the Axis powers would have been a major blow to the Allies and their ability to operate their naval forces. There was also the danger of the potential closure of the Straits of Gibraltar. Franco, however, was not persuaded and maintained an official policy of neutrality throughout the war, although Spain supported the Axis powers in various ways, probably as a result of Italy and Germany's support for Franco in the Spanish Civil War.

In 1947 Eva Peron, the wife of the Argentinian president, embarked on her European tour. The tour was essentially one of 'goodwill', but the reception, diplomatically, was mixed. George VI refused to meet her, but she was well received by Spain. On 13 July 1947 she visited Bordighera and, in honour of her visit, the seaside promenade was named Lungomare Argentina. The Pope gave her a rosary instead of a papal decoration.

A few miles up the coast from Bordighera are the Hanbury Botanical Gardens, built by the businessman, gardener and philanthropist Sir Thomas Hanbury in 1867. The gardens are situated on a steep slope that runs down to the sea very near the French–Italian border. Over several years, and with the help of his brother Daniel, who was a pharmacologist, Ludwig Winter, who was a botanist and landscape gardener, and various scientists, Sir Thomas created one of the largest gardens in Europe, containing numerous species of trees and shrubs collected by him during his many trips to the Far East. In 1912, a catalogue of the garden contained 5,800 different species, although the garden contained many others.

Sir Thomas died in 1907, but after World War I his daughter-in-law, Lady Dorothy Hanbury, carried on the work and many improvements were made. During World War II the gardens marked the front line between the US forces in France and the Germans in Italy. The war resulted in significant damage to the gardens, and in 1960 Lady Hanbury sold the gardens to the Italian state. Subsequently the University of Genoa accepted responsibility for the gardens and some restoration was undertaken. Successive generations of the Hanbury family retain the right to live in a villa within the grounds.

Over the years many members of Europe's royal families have visited the Hanbury Botanical Gardens, including Queen Victoria in 1882. In 2006 Italy submitted an unsuccessful proposal for the inclusion of the gardens on the list of UNESCO World Heritage sites. It continues, however, to be listed amongst the ten most beautiful gardens in Italy and remains a major tourist attraction.

Bordighera also became a temporary home to members of the British royal family in Victorian times, as well as the Russian nobility, who were also attracted by the climate. The latter tradition has been carried on, although now by the new wealthy pro-Putin Russians who have bought up much of the Riviera.

The old town of Bordighera sits slightly higher above the coast and still has several buildings dating from the fifteenth century, many of which were built by the Moors. Further east on the coastal approach to the town is the Casa del Mattone, a house that features in Giovanni Ruffini's romantic book *Il dottor Antonio*.[13] This novel, first published in 1855, was a major success in England.

Ruffini was born in Genoa in 1807. Trained as a lawyer, he was to pursue the cause of Italian unification, which led to his exile in France and England and being sentenced to death in absentia for being considered an enemy of the state. *Il dottor Antonio* includes his criticism of the judicial system in Italy. The novel makes a clear case for a united Italy with a sound constitutional and judicial basis. Following Italian unification in 1861 Ruffini was able to return to Italy, where he died in 1881.

The Casa del Mattone was later to play an important part in partisan activity during World War II, involving Beppe and escaped British prisoners of war.

---

[13] Giovanni Ruffini, *Doctor Antonio: A Tale of Italy* (Life Sign Press, 2011)

Casa del Mattone, partisan house near the Porcheddu villa. Ross and Bell were to hide here with partisans after German and fascist searches in the mountains. They escaped when the house was raided by fascists, but the partisans were arrested. The house featured in Giovanni Antonio's novel *Il dottor Antonio*, which was written to gain British support for Italian unification and was responsible for considerable British interest in Bordighera, where many were to settle. Ross Family Archive.

Ruffini's book and the rapid expansion of the European railway system led to a large increase in the number of British visitors to Bordighera. The popularity of Bordighera amongst the British led to many of the town's hotels having English names such as London, Grosvenor and Eden.

Bordighera was becoming the Italian equivalent of 'genteel' Brighton or Bournemouth and, following the end of World War I, there was a further migration of the English, many of whom retired to the south of France and the Italian Riviera. The Bordighera authorities have estimated that there was a period at the end of the nineteenth century when the English guests numbered as many as 3,000 whilst the local population at the time numbered 2,000. Bordighera today still has an English library, an English church and even an English cemetery.

Adjacent to the English cemetery is a well-maintained War Graves Commission cemetery designed by Sir Robert Lorimer. The cemetery contains sixty-eight British, one Indian, three West Indian and twelve Austrian burials. They had all taken part in the World War I campaign in Italy which was fought principally in the mountainous frontier area where the Italian army faced Austro-Hungarian and German forces. 2,600 British soldiers and airmen died in the campaign in Italy, and Bordighera had a military hospital to where some of the injured would have been evacuated. Those in this cemetery would probably have died of their wounds in Bordighera. A plaque on the cemetery wall reads, 'The British Empire ever remembers together with her own fallen sons those of Italy who gave their lives in the Great War 1914-1918.'

Earlier, in 1878, the English in Bordighera formed a tennis club. It still flourishes today and was the first tennis club in Italy.

Beppe, who much admired many British artists and illustrators, had found in Bordighera an ideal place to paint, well away from fascist politics.

CHAPTER VII

The Start of World War II

In 1941 Beppe began a collaboration with the children's magazine *Topolino*, for which he illustrated stories by others, as well as writing and illustrating *Il castello di San Velario* and *Il mistero degli specchi velati*. These were children's adventure stories and reflected Beppe's great imagination and perhaps escapism from the very dangerous days of his anti-fascism. The drawings for these two stories were completed in 1943 and 1944, which, for Beppe and his family, were to be particularly dangerous years. Albo d'Oro were to publish both stories, but not until July and August 1948 and therefore after Beppe's disappearance. The publication of his *I viaggi di Gulliver* was cancelled when *Topolino* ceased publication in the period 1943 to 1945.

Il castello di San Velario, written and illustrated by Beppe.

Il mistero degli specchi velati, written and illustrated by Beppe.

Beppe illustrated the series of 'Little People' for the *Corriere dei Piccoli* and *The Ring of Burma*, a novel by Renato Brunati. He also collaborated with publisher Mondadori and with Federico Pedrocchi, the comic book artist and writer. Pedrocchi had enlisted in the Italian army in 1942 and died in 1944, aged thirty-seven, in a British air raid.

Beppe illustrated the *Albi d'Oro* Mickey Mouse series and always created the front cover for *La Domenica Illustrata*. He also illustrated for the Italian newspaper *La Stampa*.

Beppe's masterpiece of illustrations was probably *The Adventures of Pinocchio* by Collodi (1942). Carlo Collodi was the pen name of Carlo Lorenzini (1826–1890), whose speciality was using allegories. Pinocchio's nose grew every time he told a lie. After unification Italian became more extensively spoken, and this popular children's book was used to extend the learning of Italian.

For his *Adventures of Pinocchio* illustrations, Beppe used only three colours: red, blue and white. He had the innovative idea of painting on light grey or beige card. This served to give a more precise emphasis to the background colour.

His illustrations also appeared in magazines like *Numero*, *Cuor d'Oro*, *L'Illustrazione del Popola* and *Scena Illustrata*. In 1941 he illustrated *Il tabù violato* for Albi Juventus, followed in 1942 by *L'invincible spada* for Il Balilla. He also illustrated schoolbooks and novels by Emilio Salgari, including *The*

Rebels of the Mountain. Salgari had written many adventure swash-bucklers until his death in Turin in 1911. He is probably the best-selling Italian author but is virtually un-known to the English-speaking world.

The Adventures of Pinocchio, illustrated by Beppe, 1942, ink on coloured paper.

Pinocchio, illustrated by Beppe, 1942, ink on coloured paper.

Beppe was particularly fascinated by literature for children. His highly acclaimed book illustrations included those for *Racconti così* by Gian Bistolfi. Bistolfi was also born in Turin and was the son of the sculptor Leonardo Bistolfi, who had appreciated Beppe's unique talent when Beppe was still a young boy. The younger Bistolfi was a famous writer and film director.

Beppe also illustrated *Tartarin of Tarascon* by Alphonse Daudet, *The Romance of Tristan and Isolde*, and *The Adventures of Baron Munchausen*. Other illustrations, not specifically intended for children, included those for *Scenic Turin* by Emilio Bruno, published in 1939 by Frassinelli, and *The Temptation of Saint Anthony* by Gustave Flaubert.

Beppe exhibited his work in many cities in Italy including Turin, Florence, Modena, San Remo, Genoa and Bordighera, earning considerable accolades and numerous gold medals and prizes. His drawings were considered masterpieces.

*

The advent of World War II and the entry of Italy on the side of the Axis powers would result in a major change in the lives of Beppe and his family. The war was to define Beppe in many ways and, although he continued painting, which by now had become a key source of income, he was determined to support the Allied cause in any way he could as a result of his anti-fascism.

Max Hastings, in his excellent World War II history *All Hell Let Loose*, commented that if Mussolini had preserved Italian neutrality in 1940, it was possible that he might have maintained his dictatorship for many years in the same way as Franco.[14] The consequences, however, of Italy aligning itself to Germany were to prove catastrophic for Italy. This decision was not supported by the majority of Italians, but the overthrow of Mussolini in 1943, far from bringing Italy some respite and the opportunity to join the Allied cause, had devastating consequences. Beppe had been right to warn against the rise of Mussolini. Nazi repression and the fear of deportation to Germany led to a dramatic growth of Italian partisan activity. By the end of the war it was estimated that there were 150,000 partisans fighting the Germans and fascists.

Perhaps the genesis of Beppe's anti-fascism and deep disdain and fear of

---

[14] Max Hastings, *All Hell Let Loose* (London: Harper Press, 2011)

Nazism lay in his experience of World War I. Once again peace in Europe was being threatened by the ambitions of two dictators, Hitler and Mussolini. In World War I it was the Austrians, aided and abetted by the Germans. Now, in World War II, it was the Germans and Austrians again, but this time supported by Mussolini dragging a largely reluctant Italy into yet another war.

Mussolini's control of the levers of power was complete, but he had not appreciated the pivotal role that the partisan movement was to play, the numbers of which increased with every atrocity committed by the fascists against any Italian who opposed them. The war-weariness of the Italian male generation of the time should not be underestimated, as they had also been committed to war in Abyssinia in pursuit of Mussolini's imperial ambitions. The lack of fight attributed to the Italians in the North African campaign may be explained by this new weariness of a senseless campaign. This was in sharp contrast to the many acts of heroism and fortitude shown by the Italian army in the Dolomites in World War I.

Porcheddu family in happier times, walking along Lungomare Argentina. The Bordighera promenade was named in honour of Eva Perón, who visited the town in 1947.
Ross Family Archive.

CHAPTER VIII

Beppe and the Resistance

During the Second World War the fascists suspected Beppe's anti-Mussolini stance. The family had now moved to a villa, Llo di Mare, on the coast east of Bordighera. It was a fairly spacious villa with a large garden and located on the main coastal road. As a result of Beppe's reputation he was questioned a number of times and the house searched. Fascist police were often posted outside the villa.

It has been estimated that the fascists had files on over 100,000 Italians that they considered to be subversives. Very few, however, were sent to prison. Often the sanction was internal exile, where suspected anti-fascists were sent to remote villages and islands in the south, prevented from travelling and required to report daily to the police. University professors were forced to swear an oath of allegiance to fascism as well as to the king.

Villa Llo di Mare, located on the coast east of Bordighera. The house of the Porcheddu family, who would shelter Ross and Bell. Ross Family Archive.

Beppe had an extensive library in the house which included a number of German books, many of which were by the country's more famous philosophers. A young German officer learnt of the existence of this library, visited Beppe and asked if he could borrow books from time to time. Despite Beppe's undoubted antipathy towards the Germans it suited him to have a German officer as a perceived friend. Beppe recognised, however, that not all Germans were Nazis, and perhaps he even took a liking to the young German officer who, had he not been conscripted, would have probably been a university lecturer.

This association was to become very useful later in the war, when the German officer may have vetoed regular searches of Beppe's house, proposed as a result of Beppe's well-known anti-fascist views. Beppe's daughter Giovanna thought that the German officer may even have warned Beppe of an impending search of the villa by the fascists.

Despite his anti-fascism, Beppe appeared to be a supporter of the monarchy. He had accepted a knighthood for his services to the arts. The king, Victor Emmanuel III, had supported Mussolini, but for pragmatic reasons, as he saw this as the best and perhaps only way of safeguarding the future of the monarchy against the rising support for communism in Europe and in particular in Italy. Giovanna remembers her father proudly wearing his miniature lapel knighthood medal.

During the war the Italian king was still Victor Emmanuel III. One day Beppe heard that the king's wife, Queen Elena of Montenegro, was passing the villa. He invited his twin daughters to mark the occasion by standing outside the villa as her carriage passed and waving at her. The queen passed and asked that her carriage be stopped. She had spotted an unusual flowering tree (a Jacaranda) and wanted to see it in more detail. Some flowering branches of the tree were cut off and the twins were able to offer them to the queen. She duly accepted and asked how many children were in the family. The next day, in a rather nice touch from the queen, a footman arrived at the villa and presented a commemorative medallion to the two girls and their brother in gratitude for the flowers. One of the medallions is still in the hands of the family.

One may wonder how Beppe's apparent support for the monarchy squared with his undoubted communist sympathies. There is no evidence that Beppe was a communist in the mould of those in Russia. He would have abhorred their treatment meted out to anyone opposed to communism and the absence of freedom of speech or expression, as well as the persecution of artists and writers. His communist leanings may have been more as a result of his concern over inequalities in Italy, creating a desire to support the disadvantaged or even for the redistribution of wealth. One must also remember that Beppe's key driver was that of anti-fascism and many of the partisans who were fighting the fascists were communists, possibly around 50% of the total partisan numbers.

Beppe's villa became a meeting place for the anti-fascists in the area. He was also to provide assistance to Jews who had been persecuted by Mussolini and were attempting to flee to France or the USA. It is against this background that one can judge the bravery of Beppe, who during the war gave considerable assistance to the partisans in the Bordighera area.

Beppe was an important member of the clandestine local National Liberation Committee. The CLN (Comitato di Liberazione Nationale) had been set up secretly by anti-fascists in German-occupied Italy with the object of helping resistance groups and co-ordinating underground activities. The CLN became a political umbrella organisation and the main representative of the Italian partisans fighting against the German occupation of Italy in the aftermath of the Italian armistice.

The CLN was a multi-party organisation, whose members were united in their anti-fascism. It was formed on 9 September 1943, following Italy's surrender to the Allies and Germany's invasion of the country. It was to lead the government of Italy from the liberation of Rome in June 1944 until the first post-war elections in 1946.

After the war Beppe was to become the president for the local branch of the committee. Giovanna, however, described her father as a somewhat reluctant chairman; Beppe had become very disillusioned with Italian post-war politics and much preferred his world of art, music and literature.

German retribution for partisan attacks in Italy was amongst the many atrocities committed by the Germans against civilians. It often followed the Roman principle of decimation, a form of military discipline where one soldier in a group of ten offenders was executed. In this case it was the male members of any village near a partisan attack who were to suffer. The German commander-in-chief in Italy, Field Marshal Kesselring, even said he would protect any officers who exceeded usual restraint in dealing with partisans.

In Venice, after the war, Kesselring was tried by a British military court for war crimes. He was arraigned on two charges: inciting German soldiers to shoot Italian civilians, and ordering the shooting of 335 Italian civilians in Rome, which became known as the Ardeatine massacre. The executions were ordered on 24 March 1944 as a reprisal following a partisan attack on

Germans in Rome the previous day. Kesselring maintained that the order to kill ten Italian civilians for each German soldier killed by partisans was 'just and lawful'.

Kesselring was found guilty on both counts on 6 May 1947 and sentenced to death. Both Churchill and Field Marshal Harold Alexander intervened in the hope that the sentence be commuted. They, and many others in the United Kingdom, felt that Kesselring had been a gallant soldier who had fought his battles fairly. Italy refused to carry out the sentence as it was in the process of abolishing the death penalty, which it regarded as a relic of Mussolini's fascist regime. Shortly afterwards, the War Office notified all commands that there should be no more death sentences and those already imposed should be commuted. Kesselring was instead sentenced to life imprisonment. He was released in 1952 on grounds of ill health and died in 1960.

The risks Beppe took were to become considerably greater when he decided to help two British army officers who had escaped from a prisoner-of-war camp in Italy, following the country's capitulation in September 1943.

CHAPTER IX

British Prisoners of War

When the Allied invasion of mainland Italy started on 3 September 1943, there were over 80,000 Allied prisoners of war in fifty-two camps across the country. Many of these had been captured in the early part of the North African campaign. By September 1943 some, therefore, had been prisoners for over three years.

Captain Michael Ross, Welch Regiment, father of the author. At university at the outbreak of war, Ross immediately volunteered for officer training along with the whole of the Loughborough Colleges 1st XV rugby team. Sadly, he was the only 'back' left alive at the end of the war.
Ross Family Archive.

Michael Ross, in his book *The British Partisan*[15] (previously published as *From Liguria with Love*), describes how the Allied prisoners of war were told by army headquarters that they were to remain in their camps and await the arrival of Allied forces who would be moving north following the Allied landings in southern Italy. The original order had come from the War Office in a coded message. Ross and other officers realised that this was an absurd order, devoid of any understanding of the situation on the ground. They knew that there was a very real danger that the retreating Germans would take any prisoners back with them to Germany.

Ross's Italian camp commandant, Lieutenant Colonel Eugenio Vicedomini, at Prigione di Guerra 49 Fontanellato, near Parma, promised that in the event of any sign of approaching Germans he would open the gates. He even ordered a wide gap to be cut in the perimeter fence to allow for a quick evacuation.

---

[15] Michael Ross, *The British Partisan* (Barnsley: Pen & Sword, 2019)

On 9 September, word came that German vehicles were approaching the camp. True to his word, the Italian commandant ordered the bugler to sound the alarm, and Ross and some 600 prisoners fled to pre-arranged locations. The Italian commandant was later to be arrested by the Germans and taken to Germany after they arrived at the camp and found it was largely empty of Allied prisoners of war. Those Allied prisoners who remained were indeed taken back to Germany for further imprisonment until the end of the war.

Having evacuated the immediate area of the camp, Ross and the other prisoners dispersed in small groups as soon as it was dark to move further away from the camp, which would soon be searched by the Germans.

As a consequence of the order to stay put in the camps, over 50,000 of the 80,000 Allied prisoners of war across Italy were taken by the Germans to camps in Germany and Poland. What happened to the remainder is not clear, but the Ministry of Defence has estimated that 11,500 escaped by crossing the Alps into Switzerland or by heading south though the German lines to rejoin Allied forces. Many others joined Italian partisan units and continued to attack the Germans and fascists. Sadly, some did not survive this most dangerous part of the war in Italy.

Ross teamed up with an officer of the Highland Light Infantry, George Bell. Both Ross and Bell had volunteered for the army at the outbreak of war. Ross had been at university, whilst Bell was a tea planter in Ceylon. They were well matched, both quiet, not given to overt display, resourceful, loyal and determined.

The options for escaping prisoners of war were to go north towards Switzerland, head south through what was still a battlefront or head west through France to neutral Spain and Gibraltar. Ross and Bell dismissed the option of Switzerland, as it would have ended with indefinite internment under Switzerland's neutrality obliga-tions, and decided on the shorter route south to Allied forces.

Ross had already escaped once

Lieutenant George Bell, Highland Light Infantry. He and Ross escaped together after the Italian Armistice. A tea planter from Ceylon, he was to return there after the war. Ross Family Archive.

before from the same prisoner-of-war camp. On 7 May 1943 Ross and a fellow officer in the Welch Regiment, Jimmy Day, hid themselves in a shallow trench that had been secretly dug in an exercise area of the camp. A game of rugby and a scrum provided the opportunity for Ross and Day to enter the trench and be covered over by boards and earth. Under cover of darkness the two men scrambled out from their hiding place, cut through the perimeter fence and began to make their way north. After ten days on the run they were recaptured on the Swiss border and returned to Fontanellato to spend thirty days in 'the Cooler', the nickname for solitary confinement.

Ross and Day's escape has been covered in a number of books by prisoners of war. A full account of how Ross and Day escaped is in Dominick Graham's book, *The Escapes and Evasions of an Obstinate Bastard*.[16] Malcolm Tudor, in his book *Beyond the Wire*,[17] covers a number of escapes, including that of Ross and Day, and records the courage of Tudor's Italian grandfather, grandmother and family, who assisted prisoners of war at great risk to themselves. Ian English, himself an escapee, edited a book which compiled the remarkable stories of several escapes from Fontanellato.[18] One of the accounts describes Ross and Day's escape, the first from the camp. English particularly emphasises the bravery and sacrifices of the Italian people, many of whom were poor peasant farmers who gave the escapees shelter, food and clothing at great personal risk to themselves.

On this second escape on 9 September 1943, following the Italian armistice, Ross and Bell initially headed south but, finding the area too heavily occupied by the Germans, decided to turn northwest with the intention of keeping to the mountains parallel to the coast, moving through Liguria and France to neutral Spain and Gibraltar.

Max Hastings, in his book *All Hell Let Loose*, writes about the escaping prisoners of war after the Italian surrender. He particularly comments on the help that the Italian people gave to the escaping Allied prisoners. The risks were considerable and included the destruction of their homes and often death. This bravery of the Italian people represented one of the noblest aspects of Italy's unhappy part in the war.

Whilst on the run, Ross and Bell received considerable help from local

---

[16] Dominick Graham, *The Escapes and Evasions of an Obstinate Bastard* (Windsor: Wilton65, 2000)
[17] Malcolm Tudor, *Beyond the Wire* (Newtown: Emilia, 2009)
[18] Ian English, *Home by Christmas* (privately published, 1997)

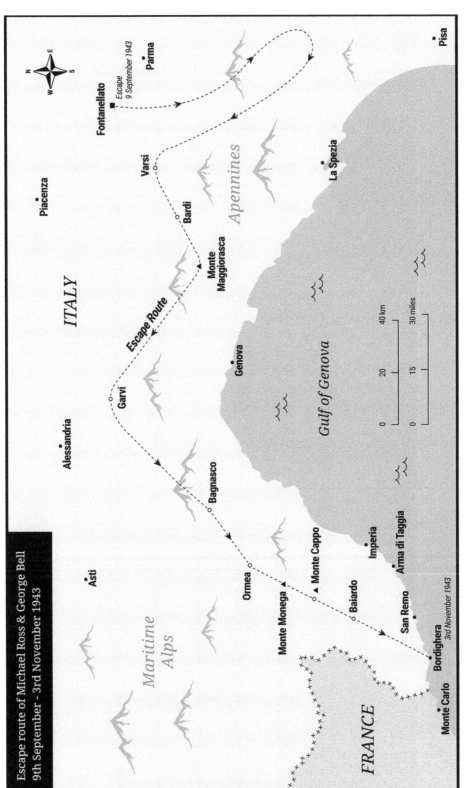

Escape route of Michael Ross and George Bell, 9 September to 3 November 1943.

Renato Brunati, partisan commander and friend of Beppe. Executed by the Germans in 1944.

Italians. This consisted of food, shelter and often clothes, as the mountain range of the Apennines was becoming increasingly cold with winter approaching. The threat of retribution from the Germans against the local population, had they been discovered helping escaped prisoners of war, was ever present, and Ross and Bell always kept on the move.

Travelling due west, they were in Liguria and only twenty miles from the French border within several weeks. It was December, and the snow and cold in the mountains was sapping their strength, so they decided to descend towards the coast and below the snowline. They reached the village of Baiardo, ten miles from the coast. Here they encountered Renato Brunati, and this was to change the entire course of events for them.

Brunati was initially suspicious, but his manner changed when he realised that they were British officers. He was the leader of a group of eight

Baiardo, Liguria, a medieval village 3,000 feet above sea level. The location of Ross and Bell's first encounter with partisans and Renato Brunati. They had hoped that Ross and Bell were SOE officers and would bring them some weapons.

partisans, which included his companion Lina Maiffret. They had all escaped arrest in their home town of San Remo.

It was reassuring for Ross to come across partisans, even if they only had one rifle between them. Brunati, however, had hoped that Ross and Bell had arrived to equip them with weapons. When it became clear that all they wanted to do was catch up on sleep, Brunati commented that, if all the British were like these two, victory would be some way off.

Brunati departed to try to find a guide to take Ross and Bell through the German-patrolled French border. Unsuccessful, he instead found a fisherman who offered to take them to Corsica, which had been liberated in October 1943. They leapt at this opportunity, as a sea journey of some 125 miles might be less dangerous than getting through German lines.

CHAPTER X

Beppe Meets Ross and Bell

Brunati had discussed the Corsica plan with his trusted friend, Beppe, who was now the head of CLN, the clandestine anti-fascist organisation. Beppe and his family were still living in the villa Llo di Mare in Arziglia, a small town on the coast just east of Bordighera. Beppe suggested that the two officers move to his villa whilst the partisans made final arrangements with the fisherman.

The two escapees arrived at Beppe's villa and were immediately greeted by the whole family. Ross and Bell had previously heard of Beppe from the partisans and fully understood the risk that he was taking for himself and his family by sheltering them in his villa. Ross therefore hoped they would soon be on their way to Corsica.

After three days Brunati and Maiffret returned with the disappointing news that the fisherman had left the area. Ross and Bell returned to the plan to cross the French border and left with the partisans for the mountains.

Over the next two weeks the Germans increased their patrols in the mountains where the partisans were operating, so Brunati suggested moving to his own villa on the coast. It was situated close to Beppe's villa, so Brunati would be able to consult him.

They walked through the night, arriving at the villa in the early morning. It was close to a railway line but also dangerously close to the main road. Brunati was well known for his anti-fascist views, and Ross and Bell immediately looked around the villa and garden to plan their escape routes should they become necessary. A plaque on one of the walls recorded that the author Giovanni Ruffini wrote *Il dottor Antonio* whilst staying at the villa. Set in the 1840s, the book had been a great success in England and, as mentioned earlier, is credited with a major influx of the English to visit or live in Bordighera. The villa, Casa Mattone of the novel, still exists in its distinctive red brick colour.

At midday, on the first morning at 'Casa Mattone', there was a loud knock on the door. 'Carabinieri,' Maiffret whispered to Ross and Bell.

The two escapees quickly gathered the few belongings they had and made their way to a nearby railway tunnel, where they were able to hide.

After several hours and hearing nothing they went back to the villa. It was deserted, with no sign of Brunati or Maiffret. Confirming their worst fears, a trusted neighbour of Brunati told them that the couple had been arrested.

Beppe had also heard the news and had quickly arranged for two partisans, Vincenzo Gismondi and Federico Assandria, to take Ross and Bell to a safe house in the mountains. They set off together immediately. Gismondi and Assandria were being hunted by the fascists and needed to escape as well, so now the plan for all four of them to escape by boat to

Vincenzo Gismondi on the run in the Apennines after the discovery of the aborted attempt to row to Corsica with Ross and Bell. Ross Family Archive.

Federico Assandria after miraculously surviving a German firing squad. He had also tried to escape by boat to Corsica with Ross and Bell. After the war he emigrated to Venezuela, where he was to run a successful business. Ross Family Archive.

Corsica was back on, and with a greater urgency.

Whilst in the mountains they sheltered in some deserted huts, and Beppe and his family visited them with food and drink.

A boat was located, locked in a hut on a beach. Ross and the others made their way to the beach, by now having been joined by Elio Muraglio, another partisan being hunted by the fascists. They broke into the hut and carried the boat down to the water's edge. The plan was to row out for about a mile and then start a small outboard that Gismondi had acquired. The boat was launched and they rowed away from the shore. They were euphoric with their success, but the elation was not to last. Water started entering the boat through cracks in the dry warped wooden boards. Bailing out proved futile and the boat began to sink. Fortunately, with the assistance of a sea swell, they managed to return to shore just before the boat finally sank. They quickly dispersed, and Ross and Bell went to Beppe's villa to ask for his help once again.

Beppe took them in without hesitation, and they remained with the family over that Christmas period. They also heard the very happy news that Brunati and Maiffret had been released.

Ross was increasingly worried about the safety of Beppe and his family, as they had now been there for three weeks. Fortuitously, Brunati and Maiffret visited, so they departed together for the mountains.

On reaching a house owned by Maiffret they were in for a shock. It had been ransacked by the Germans. The area was clearly compromised, so they continued higher up into the mountains, where they were relieved to find the rest of the partisans. Whilst they were in the mountains, Beppe and his family continued to visit and provide everyone with food.

Brunati and Maiffret now left for San Remo to meet other partisans. Two days later, and again at great risk, Beppe and his family visited with food supplies, but also with the alarming news that Brunati and Maiffret had been rearrested and were being interrogated. With these arrests, Ross, Bell

Partisans of Garibaldi Division in the hills above Bordighera. Distinguishable by their red scarves. Communists, some of whom had gained operational experience fighting in the International Brigade in the Spanish Civil War. Ross and Bell were to join them.

and the partisans were now at great risk. Beppe secretly proposed to Ross that they should return to his villa until they could decide what to do next. No one was to know of this plan, so Ross and Bell's cover was that they would walk to the border and cross into France. Following farewells to the partisans, they started to walk west towards the border but then changed course and headed back to Beppe's villa.

Some days later two of the partisans who had tried to get to Corsica with Ross and Bell, Gismondi and Assandria, arrived at the villa to tell Beppe that two British officers had been captured by the Germans on the French border and shot. The partisans had assumed that it must have been Ross and Bell. Gismondi and Assandria were clearly very upset, and it was hard for the Porcheddu family to resist allaying their fears with the information that Ross and Ball were safely upstairs. Security considerations precluded the family from telling anyone the whereabouts of Ross and Bell. They had to play out their sorrow convincingly.

Ross and Bell became part of the daily lives of the household, though the danger of discovery was never far away. Life was structured with Beppe organising the study and music periods for the twins, Giovanna and Amalia, now eighteen, and Bitita, sixteen. The conversation at table was stimulating as all the family were well read, particularly Beppe. The mood was generally good, but on occasion Beppe would enter a somewhat sombre mood and his depression would cast a shadow over the family. Beppe, for political reasons, had isolated himself from much of the community around him and rarely indulged in social activities. He was very much alone with his responsibilities, which must have weighed heavily on his mind.

Ross and Bell were to remain at the villa for three months. A secret room behind a large wardrobe provided refuge for them from visiting fascists, who

Ross and Bell's successful hiding place in the villa. Even when the fascists searched the house, it was never discovered. Ross Family Archive.

always suspected Beppe's involvement with the partisans. It was in this room that Ross and Bell hid when the German officer visited to borrow Beppe's illustrated German books, some of which Beppe used for inspiration in his drawings. The hideout was put to the test on another occasion when fascist police searched the house again, as Beppe continued to be under suspicion.

In *The British Partisan* Ross describes another occasion when Beppe risked his own life and that of his family to give refuge to anti-fascists. One morning two ladies knocked on the villa door. They were the wife and daughter of a prominent anti-fascist, Concetto Marchesi, an old friend of Beppe.

Marchesi was born on 1 February 1878 in Catania and died on 12 February 1957. He was the rector of Padua University, and in December 1943 he called on all students to join the partisans. He was a Marxist and a key member of the Italian communist party. He immediately went on the run as he would have been arrested by the fascists.

Marchesi fled to Switzerland in February 1944, where he worked with the Allies in organising the supply of arms and ammunition to the partisans. He also ensured that supplies were directed to the Garibaldi division of the partisans. These were communist partisans, and Marchesi had visions of an Italian revolution to bring the communists to power. After the war he was to become a prominent Italian politician, representing the communist party in the Constituent Assembly from 1946 to 1948 and in the Chamber of Deputies from 1948 to 1957.

As a result of Marchesi's actions his wife and daughter were now in immediate danger, and Beppe and Rita had no hesitation in taking them in. All this posed a considerable risk to Beppe and his family, but one which Beppe he felt he had to take.

It was clearly vital that these two new house guests know nothing of the presence of two British officers. Despite the difficulties, the two parties were able to live under the same roof for two weeks without the ladies knowing that the officers existed. The ladies' departure to a permanent place of hiding in the village of Apricale, in the hills behind Bordighera, was a great relief to Ross and Bell.

Shortly afterwards the fascist police decided to take action. Beppe was placed under house arrest and ordered to report for further questioning in Imperia, the provincial capital. Alarmingly, on arrival for questioning Beppe caught sight of Brunati, who was also being held there. Brunati, by way of a secret sign, was able to indicate to Beppe that he had not revealed their association.

During several hours of questioning, Beppe successfully refuted all the allegations put to him, and as the fascists had no evidence Beppe was released to return to the villa.

CHAPTER XI

Partisan Activity Increases

The Porcheddu family and Ross and Bell were able to listen to the BBC World Service when finally the exciting news came of the opening up of the second front and D-Day on 6 June 1944. Military activity in the area increased with the Germans expanding operations against the partisans and with the Allies attacking German positions and their navy.

The Germans reinforced their beach defences in the Bordighera area as they expected an Allied landing along that area of the coast. Instead, later that year, on 15 August, the US 7th Army landed in the south of France between Cannes and St Tropez. This was Operation Anvil (later Dragoon) and was one of the most successful and significant operations in Europe. It was also marked by the relatively few casualties suffered in the amphibious landings.

Earlier, following the Allied victory in North Africa, the Allies had started to plan for further operations against the Axis powers. An invasion of Sicily and then mainland Italy became the top priority, but other options, including a landing in southern France, were also being considered. The attraction of an invasion of southern France, coupled with an Allied invasion of northern France, would have been to stretch German defences to a point that would have left them extremely vulnerable. It was not, however, until after the successful landings in Normandy in June 1944, and the capture of Rome, that the Allies had sufficient landing craft and supplies available to support Operation Dragoon.

During Operation Dragoon, as the Allies moved eastwards toward the Italian–French border, the noise of the battle could be clearly heard in Bordighera. It was at that point that a trusted friend of Beppe who worked in the local government offices brought news that he had seen a secret list of people to be arrested and held as hostages by the Germans and the fascists. Beppe's name was at the top of the list. There was no time to lose.

Ross and Bell's presence increased the danger to the Porcheddu family, and the two of them immediately made for the mountains in order to try to join the partisans once again. The villa had to be evacuated and Beppe

Giovanna Porcheddu, the author's mother. Giovanna and Michael Ross were to marry in October 1946 at the Porcheddu villa. Ross Family Archive.

decided that, for their safety, the family should be split up to hide with different friends. Giovanna and Amalia hid in the villa of friends on a hill overlooking Bordighera, from which Monet had painted his famous landscape of the town.

For Michael Ross the departure was particularly difficult, as he realised that he had fallen in love with Giovanna. The safety of the Porcheddu family was paramount, and remaining in the coastal area would be very dangerous for him and Bell as well as for the Porcheddu family. Ross wondered if he would ever see them again, but, most importantly, Giovanna.

Moving up into the mountains, Ross and Bell had to take evasive action several times to avoid German patrols. On one occasion they found themselves within feet of a dozing German sentry. They pressed on, wondering if they would ever find any partisans, when suddenly a young man armed with a pistol sprang out from behind some bushes and challenged them. They attempted to explain themselves, but he kept his pistol aimed at them and directed them to a hut.

Inside was a group of ten armed men around a log fire. At last they had met up with the partisans. The group was from the Garibaldi Brigade and their red scarves marked them out as communists.

Stone huts near Baiardo: partisan hideout where Ross and Bell rejoined the partisan group
after the Porcheddu family were forced to abandon the villa. Ross and Bell made it a rule never
to sleep in the same place for more than one night consecutively. Ross Family Archive.

There was an uneasy, suspicious atmosphere, and Ross and Bell wished
they had avoided this particular encounter. Bruno, the leader, suspected
they were German spies and started to question them. Revealing the help
given to them from Beppe and the Porcheddu family might have cleared
them, but doing so could have jeopardised the safety of the family.

Dissatisfied with their inadequate explanations, Bruno pointed his pistol
at Ross and Bell and coldly told them that, in the morning, if they did not
explain fully where they had been, they would be shot.

That night, guarded by armed partisans, Ross and Bell lay awake
contemplating the approach of dawn. This would indeed be an ironic way
for their lives to end.

Dawn broke, and Bruno entered the room where Ross and Bell had been
guarded overnight. He looked stern and was undoubtedly determined to
find out who had been sheltering them. Pointing his pistol, he ordered them
outside into the bright sunlight.

There they saw another armed partisan whom they did not recognise.
He was introduced as Vitto. This was Giuseppe Vittorio Guglielmo
(1916–2002). He was the commander of the Garibaldi division and had
fought in the International Brigade in Spain.

Vitto and Bruno were soon in deep conversation. Both had serious looks
on their faces, and Ross feared the worst. Vitto then came over to Ross and
said that he was the leader of another partisan group which included two

Americans. It was clear that the Americans would now be used to interrogate Ross and Bell to establish the truth. They could hardly believe their good fortune.

It was a two-day trek to Vitto's unit further up in the mountains. They were accompanied by Bruno, who was ever surly. On arrival they met the two American pilots who had parachuted from their plane after being shot down. After a short discussion the US pilots were able to reassure the partisans that Ross and Bell were indeed British officers. Bruno then departed back to his unit. Ross and Bell were glad to see the back of him, as he had personally executed several captured fascists.

German forces in the Bordighera and French border area mainly comprised the 34th Infantry Division commanded by General Theo-Helmut Lieb. This included three regiments, the 80th, the

Partisan commander 'Vitto' Guglielmo, born in San Remo in 1916. Fought in the International Brigade in the Spanish Civil War and commanded the partisan Garibaldi Division in northern Italy. He interrogated Ross and Bell, who were suspected to be German spies.
Copyright Alzani Editore.

107th and the 253rd, each containing two battalions and also artillery and divisional support units. It represented a formidable and battle-hardened enemy force, but the partisans were still able to harass and attack the Germans whenever the opportunity arose in typical guerrilla fashion.

Ross's group had additional help from a Special Operations Executive officer, Captain Robert Bentley.[19] Bentley had been inserted by sea on the coast near Bordighera from a Royal Navy submarine with his radio operator on 6 January 1945. He was tasked with arranging the delivery of arms to the partisans and radioing back enemy positions and movements.

The weapons were to be delivered by rubber dinghies launched from a submarine. It was planned for the weapons to be landed on a beach at Arma di Taggia, a few miles east from Bordighera. As part of the weapons delivery plan Ross and Bell, along with the two American pilots, would escape by boarding the submarine at the end of the operation.

---

[19] Obituary, Robert Bentley, *The Daily Telegraph*, 1 April 2013

On the appointed night, just as the partisans and the Allied officers were nearing the beach, flares suddenly illuminated the whole of the beach area and German coastal guns opened up, firing out to sea. In the confusion everyone escaped, but it was a disastrous setback. At the time Ross thought that the submarine had given away its position through engine noise, but there was to be another explanation.

A second attempt ten days later ended in similar failure. Despite this, Bentley and the partisans were determined to try again. The supply of arms and ammunition was vital to them and fully justified the risks.

On the third attempt Ross and the partisans were stopped by a partisan acting as a forward scout before they could get to their beach positions. The Germans were lying in wait in ambush positions on exactly the route they were to take. How could the Germans have known of the timings and route in such detail? The partisans concluded that an informer must have tipped off the Germans.

An investigation was held and it concluded that one of the female partisans, Olga, must have betrayed them to the Germans. She claimed to be Yugoslav and was used by the partisans to befriend Germans and gain information. None of the partisans had been captured after the second attempt to meet up with the submarine, and only Olga had had subsequent contact with the Germans. The partisans decided that she must have been acting as a double agent. There could only be one outcome.

Two partisans arrived at Ross and Bell's base in the mountains to explain what they had decided. Olga was to be told that Ross and Bell wished to speak to her about the information that she had gained from the Germans. The appalling scenario that was to be enacted later that day left Ross numb. The waiting was harrowing. Three hours later Olga and two partisans approached Ross and Bell's hut. A single shot rang out and she slumped to the ground. Ross and the partisans hastily buried her in a shallow grave. A small pair of boots, thrown to one side, was the only reminder of this tragedy.

In the hut that night no one had much appetite for food and there was little conversation. The young partisan who had carried out the act sat shivering and crying. He was an unlikely killer, an ordinary young man who had worked in a bank.

It was clear that Olga's recent treachery had not been confined to the attempted arms delivery. The next day the Germans started a major operation against the partisans. They must have known exactly where the group was hiding, as the huts they were using were suddenly attacked by the

Germans. A number of partisans, along with Ross and Bell, managed to escape and hide in woods higher up the mountain. Several partisans were killed and others captured only to be summarily executed.

Ross's group quickly reorganised and moved to a new location. There they met up again with Captain Bentley, and it was clear that there would be no more attempted arms deliveries for the time being. Ross and the others therefore discussed an alternative plan of escape by finding a boat and rowing to France, which was now held by the Allies. The battlefront was now only fifteen miles away, lying roughly along the French–Italian border stretching from the Alps to the coast. The Germans were along the Italian side and heavily dug in. Getting through the defensive line was going to be extremely difficult, but an escape by sea was considered slightly less dangerous. Ross's group was now up to five, Ross, Bell and the two American pilots having been joined by a Free French pilot whose plane had also been shot down.

The next few weeks proved to be the most dangerous that Ross and Bell had spent with the partisans. They continued to attack the Germans and fascists, but the partisans were taking significant casualties. Ross was impressed with the partisans, whom he considered well-trained and very courageous. Capture meant execution, and a similar fate might await Ross and Bell, who, dressed in civilian clothes, could expect to be treated as spies. The two of them had decided they would never stay in the same place for more than one night.

On one fateful occasion the partisans, tired of moving, stayed in the same hut for a second night. Ross and Bell, keeping to their rule not to spend more than one night in the same location, departed and said they would meet up with the rest of the group in the morning. They crossed the valley and settled down for the night under some bushes.

At dawn the silence was suddenly broken by the sound of three explosions, followed by shouting and gunfire. Finally, the firing stopped and all was quiet.

It would have been too dangerous for Ross and Bell to move during daylight, so at dusk they made their way carefully back to the hut. There was no sign of movement as they approached. Their worst fears were confirmed. All the partisans were lying dead on the floor. There was nothing they could do for them now, and so they immediately left the area.

CHAPTER XII

Another Attempted Escape

Ross and Bell decided they must press on with their plan to row to France. With the help of partisans they moved from the mountains to the coast near the German line on the French–Italian border. The area was being shelled by Allied artillery and many coastal buildings had been evacuated. Two boats were found by the partisans in the coastal town of Vallecrosia, located between Bordighera and the Italian border town of Ventimiglia. Four Italians who were being hunted by the fascists also joined them, as this might be their last chance to escape.

Getting the boats through a railway viaduct guarded by Italian militiamen under German command was not going to be easy. Fortunately, an Italian who was sympathetic to the resistance had arranged to be on duty on the night in question.

They managed to get the boats through the viaduct into the water and they all scrambled aboard. Ross, Bell and the partisans had made a previous attempt two days earlier, which had ended in failure when the boat was swamped by high waves and they all nearly drowned. On this second attempt, however, the two boats were launched safely into a calmer sea.

They estimated that Monte Carlo could be reached in seven hours, and well before dawn. They were able to make good progress and encountered no enemy patrols. On arrival at the entrance to Monte Carlo harbour they were challenged by a French sentry. Their jubilant response was something none of them would ever forget. After nearly two and a half years of imprisonment, being on the run and being sheltered and helped by Beppe, Ross and Bell were finally safe.

After breakfast in the Bristol Hotel they were debriefed on their last incredible eighteen months and then driven to Nice. Ross and Bell were then flown to Naples to join a convoy returning to Britain, and their first sight of home was the Clyde estuary out of which Ross had sailed in 1941. Ross was subsequently recognised for his escape activities by the award of mention in despatches.[20]

---

[20] Citation, Lt MP Ross, Welch Regt

*

Not all went well for the partisans Ross and Bell had left behind. Several were captured and executed. Particularly sad for Ross and Bell was the execution of Renato Brunati, the first partisan they had met, who was also a good friend of Beppe. He was arrested in 1944, taken to a prison in Genoa and, together with other hostages, executed by firing squad. Brunati's companion, Lina Meifrett, was also arrested, but instead was deported to Germany, where she suffered the horrors of a labour camp before finally escaping and making her way back to Italy.

Vincenzo Gismondi, Elio Muraglio and Federico Assandria, who had attempted to row to Corsica with Ross and Bell, all survived the war. Assandria, though, had a miraculous escape. He was captured with five other partisans in the Piedmont region and taken to some woods to be shot. The executions were carried out, and all but Assandria died instantly. He fell to the ground, shot in the shoulder and neck. He was left for dead along with the others. But he was not fatally wounded and that night summoned the strength to escape. He recovered, rejoined the partisans and later served in an Italian artillery regiment.

Gismondi crossed the lines, enlisted in the Italian division of the British 8th Army and fought in the successful operation against the Germans on the Gothic Line. After the war he returned to the family home in Bordighera.

Assandria emigrated to Venezuela, but he, Muraglio and Gismondi were to remain close friends of the Porcheddu family.

On a hill overlooking the port of Bordighera is a memorial to the partisans who were executed or killed in action. At the top of the list is Renato Brunati. Nearly all the names on the list were known to Ross and Bell.

The contribution of the partisans has often been underestimated. They kept as many as seven German divisions away from defending Germany and were also responsible for the surrender of two full German divisions, which led directly to the collapse of the German forces in and around Genoa, Turin and Milan. By May 1944 it was estimated that there were 70,000 to 80,000 partisans, of which about half were in the Garibaldi divisions and brigades. There were around 14,200 partisans in Liguria, where Ross and Bell were operating.

The post-war Italian government listed partisan casualties as 35,828 killed in action or executed, with a further 21,168 seriously injured or disabled. Other accounts have put partisan casualties as high as 50,000 killed. Another 32,000 Italian partisans had been killed abroad in the Balkans and France. Italian civilians killed in reprisals by German or fascist forces amounted to 9,980.

Although many fascists saw themselves as the sons of Garibaldi, so did many anti-fascists. In the Spanish Civil War supporters of Mussolini fought in support of Franco whilst the opposing International Brigade included the

Memorial to partisans killed in action, Bordighera. Renato Brunati's name heads the list. He was the first partisan whom Ross and Bell encountered. Ross Family Archive.

Garibaldi Brigade, which was to become a major force amongst the partisans fighting the Germans in Italy.

Although Churchill was against any alignment with communists, for practical reasons it was in Britain's interests to make use of them against the Germans. It was also important because the Mediterranean was a key channel to much of Britain's overseas territories and interests.

The fall of Mussolini and the subsequent armistice resulted in Germany sending reinforcements to Italy and occupying much of the northern and central parts of the country. This led directly to the setting up of Italian resistance groups.

Initially Britain hoped to keep the king and Marshal Badoglio, the prime minister, in power in Italy after the fall of Mussolini as a counter against the communists, despite widespread Italian opposition. As with Greece and Yugoslavia, the fear was that the country would fall into communist hands.

The partisans had no love for the king or Badoglio because of their association with fascism. Allied involvement in Italy was limited to defeating the Germans, and the Allies had little interest in social change in the country, particularly if it led to instability. This was the very opposite of the aspirations of the partisans, who wanted a complete clear-out of the fascists. The Allies and the resistance were therefore generally suspicious of each other, but the former realised that the partisans were extremely useful and therefore should not be alienated. As the war continued in Italy the CLN became increasingly well organised and a close relationship with the resistance became a vital goal for the Allies.

Around 50% of the partisans came from the Garibaldi Brigades, and therefore the communists were moving towards a potentially strong position in the lead-up to a post-war Italy. This would later lead to the British policy of the disarming of the partisans. After the war, in the Italian elections of 1948, the communist party used the face of Garibaldi as its flag.

There are many amusing stories attached to the partisans. One concerns the family recollections of the late Antonio Carluccio, the well-known chef and restaurateur, as told to the *Sunday Times Magazine*. During the war his family lived in Castelnuovo Belbo, a village in Piedmont. Despite the war in Europe Carluccio describes his village as a haven of tranquillity and peace. The village partisans decreed that each family could only own one pig, and if a family owned more than one the additional pigs were to be given to the partisans. This was an unpopular ruling for Carluccio's father, the station master of the local train stop, as he owned a second pig, which he had raised and fed for many months. Late one night he and other men from the village gathered in the railway station waiting room, slaughtered the pig and divided it up amongst the families. With considerable satisfaction they were able to ensure that this pig, at least, did not go to the partisans.

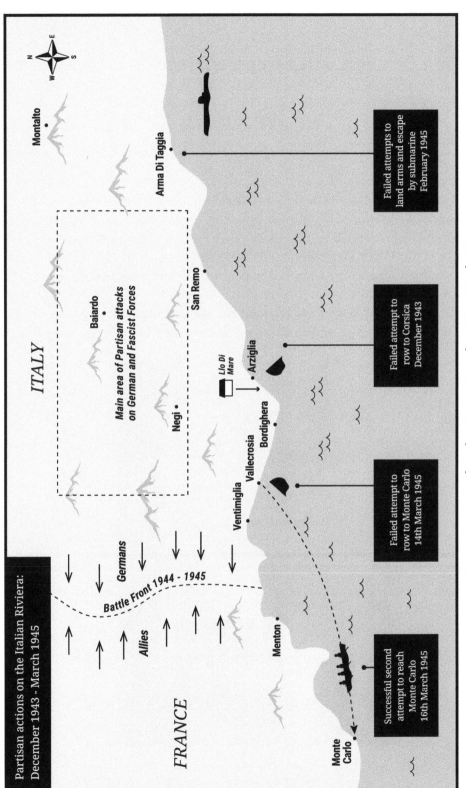

Partisan actions on the Italian Riviera, December 1943 to March 1945.

CHAPTER XIII

The War Ends

Beppe and the whole of the Porcheddu family were incredibly lucky and survived the war. Many British prisoners of war had mixed fortunes. Those who had remained in their camps after the armistice, including many officers of the Welch Regiment, were taken to Germany by the retreating German army, where they remained in prisoner-of-war camps until the end of the war.

After a period of leave Ross rejoined the Welch Regiment, and a short time later hostilities ceased in Europe. He then had the opportunity to

Ross's return to the Porcheddu villa Llo di Mare after the war and reunion with the Porcheddu family. Ross Family Archive.

Double wedding at Llo di Mare, 11 October 1946. Ross Family Archive.

Author's mother and father, 11 October 1946. Giovanna Porcheddu and Michael Ross's wedding day at the Porcheddu villa, Bordighera. Ross Family Archive.

return to Italy in 1946 for a staff appointment. There was to be a joyful reunion with the Porcheddu family and in particular with Giovanna, with whom he had fallen in love. The two were married later that year. Giovanna's twin sister, Amalia, was also to marry a British officer, Captain Philippe Garigue (1917–2008) of the Royal Fusiliers, in a double ceremony conducted in Beppe's villa, Llo di Mare.

Garigue had been appointed as the post-war military governor of the area and got to know Beppe because of his influential position in the community. In post-war Italy, the long-disputed French–Italian border had once again come under the spotlight, and it was proposed that the Italian coastal area of Ventimiglia be annexed to France. It is understood that Garigue was involved in the successful negotiations to maintain the status quo in the Ventimiglia area although, under the Treaty of Paris in 1947, France acquired the Italian border areas of Tende, La Brigue, Mont Chaberton and the lake of Mont-Cenis. There is still an ongoing and unresolved issue over the exact demarcation of the French–Italian border at the top of Mont Blanc.

In his book *The British Partisan*, Ross was to acknowledge the very significant and brave contribution made by Beppe to the Allied cause and to the resistance against fascism. A certificate from Field Marshal Alexander to

Beppe to thank him for his contribution to the Allied cause, whilst appreciated, could not reflect his courage and the risks he took.

Michael Ross died in 2012, and his obituary in the *Daily Telegraph* describes his amazing story and the courage of Beppe and his family as well as the many other Italians who helped him.[21]

In 2015 Grub Street published *The Daily Telegraph Military Obituaries, Book Three*. The book contains the Michael Ross obituary and, in the introduction, David Twiston Davies describes the Ross obituary as 'the most charming tale' in the book.[22]

An Italian publication of 2015, *Quando fischiava il vento*,[23] which describes the partisan war in northwest Italy, includes a chapter on Ross and his time with the partisans. The chapter is entitled 'Diary of a Welshman' and includes an interview with Ross.

Another publication on partisan activities, Giuseppe Fiorucci's *Gruppo Sbarchi Vallecrosia*, describes the escape by boat of Ross, Bell and others from Vallecrosia to Monte Carlo.[24] The Gruppo Sbarchi Vallecrosia was a small partisan group based in Vallecrosia, a coastal town west of Bordighera. The group concentrated on helping Allied prisoners of war and Jews escape from Italy, often by boat.

Ross and Bell would be forever grateful for the risks that the Italian people and in particular Beppe and his family took for them. After the war Ross became a supporter of the Monte San Martino Trust. The charity today supports the education of young Italians descended from families that helped escaped British prisoners of war.

---

[21] Obituary, Michael Ross, *The Daily Telegraph*, 15 April 2012
[22] David Twiston Davies, *The Daily Telegraph Military Obituaries, Book Three* (London: Grub Street, 2015)
[23] Graziella Colombini (ed.), *Quando fischiava il vento* (Pinerolo: Alzani, 2015)
[24] Giuseppe Fiorucci, *Gruppo Sbarchi Vallecrosia* (Italy: Magic Mouse, 2006)

CHAPTER XIV

Beppe's War Account

In 2020 a manuscript was brought to the attention of the author by a group of Italian historians. These historians were researching the war efforts by the partisans in the province of Liguria, which included the Bordighera area.

The manuscript is lodged in the archive of the Historical Institute of the Resistance in the University of Imperia. It consists of five pages, handwritten by Beppe, giving an account of his activities with the partisans and his sheltering of Ross, Bell and the wife and daughter of Concetto Marchesi.

It is not known for whom the account was written, and it is undated and bears no signature. Although it was unsigned, the content, which includes events, dates and personalities, is unmistakably written by Beppe. Additionally, the author has compared the handwriting to other letters by Beppe in his possession, so there is no doubt as to its authenticity.

The historians had transcribed the account, and the author has translated the content into English. Beppe writes:

The anti-fascist and anti-German movement in the Bordighera area was led by Renato Brunati and myself simultaneously but independently, without even knowing each other, but in 1940 we met and on impulse we combined our aims and our actions, linked as we were in our intellectual and artistic interests.

The real partisan action began after the fateful 8 September 1943 (the Italian armistice), when Brunati and Lina Maiffret organised the first group of partisans immediately after the German occupation and moved to the mountains on the French–Italian border, where they accumulated weapons and materials in the village of Baiardo in a house belonging to Lina Maiffret. The house served as a headquarters in the mountains, whilst on the coast my house in Arziglia on the Via Aurelia provided a meeting place for the partisans.

During the heavy rainfall in September and October 1943 the transport of arms and ammunition was particularly difficult and it became necessary for Brunati and me to take circuitous routes in order to avoid enemy patrols. We also needed to avoid contact with local people, who could not necessarily be trusted to be discreet or could even be informers. Our partisans needed to be ever alert in the areas of Negi, Monte Caggio and Baiardo.

As our numbers increased it was necessary to form a committee in San Remo and therefore contact was made with Dr Pigati, who was a fervent opponent of fascism and an active and courageous supporter, both in his office and in the Red Cross clinic.

With the help of this ally and me, food and money flowed regularly to Baiardo by way of the cable car to Monte Bignone. A valuable contribution was made to this dangerous work by a local cook and a waiter from a restaurant in Monte Bignone who assisted in the transportation of the supplies at great risk to themselves. Blankets, provisions and materials given by partisan supporters were brought to my house and then transported to the hideout in Baiardo with the help of a very active partisan, Giacometti from Ventimiglia.

Of course, it was impossible for us as leaders and for the partisans to avoid dangerous situations. Both skill and audacity were required, although on one occasion there was an encounter between two German officers, journalists and Brunati and Maiffret. A heated exchange ensued with our partisans predicting the defeat of the Axis powers, all the more dangerous as the two were wearing backpacks full of dynamite.

The partisan group now numbered about 40 and were equipped with 30 rifles, 5 machine guns, numerous bombs and good reserves of ammunition. Towards the middle of November two English officers, who had escaped from a PoW camp, arrived exhausted in Baiardo. They were looked after by our men in one of the safe houses. A plan was hatched for them to escape to Corsica by boat, but this first attempt had to be aborted as the fisherman who would lead this then vanished. The two Englishmen were brought by the partisans to my house in Arziglia under the noses of the Germans. From there they moved to the house of Brunati, located on the coast at the Madonna della Ruota. Whilst they were there a sudden surprise search by the fascist police led to the arrest of Brunati and Maiffret. The two British officers, however, had escaped and came to my house where they were to remain for 15 days.

On 22 December Brunati and Maiffret were released due to insufficient evidence and they returned to Baiardo, to where the British officers had already returned. A new attempt to escape to Corsica was organised in my house with the help of Bordighera partisans Vincenzo Gismondi, Federico Assandria and Elio Muraglio. A boat was stolen from the Donegani family villa on the coast and equipped with an outboard purchased with Giacometti's funds. After a short stay at my house to make final preparations, the two Englishmen and the three partisans moved to the shore and got into the boat successfully despite the heavy presence of the Germans in the area. The boat, however, started taking in water only 200 metres from the shore. With considerable difficulty the party all managed to return to the shore with the boat and moved to my house to recover, all soaking wet.

Gismondi was arrested shortly afterwards and this alarmed all of the partisans, and the two Englishmen moved to a hut in Negi, where they remained hidden for a few weeks. Unfortunately, on 14 February 1944, Brunati and Maiffret were arrested by the fascists following information provided by Garzo, a partisan traitor and former Blackshirt, who had returned to the fascists following a break-up with Brunati and Maiffret. The arrests would have led to immediate execution but for the intervention of a well-intentioned official who suspended the sentences. He would have succeeded completely had not the cowardly official Bussi transferred the two partisans to the German SS. Sadly, we know that Brunati and Maiffret were brutally tortured. Brunati was then shot whilst Maiffret was deported to Germany, where she was imprisoned for 10 months. She is now safely in Italy, which is miraculous.

In October 1943 I was contacted by Dr Ronga of San Remo to ask if I would form the Liberation Committee in Bordighera. I contacted Luigi Punzi, General Pognisi, Don Pellorese and Dr Marchesi, but due to the death of Punzi and with Pognisi only part-time in the area, the organisation never really formed. Later Dr Marchesi, having gathered additional support, urged me again to set up a new committee, but the presence in my house of the two English officers and my work with the partisans precluded me from taking an official position. I had also promised Brunati and Maiffret to help the two British officers.

Gino, a liaison officer with the Allies, had landed in Arziglia several times, and my home was selected to house a radio transmitter in order to send reports across the border. Then two days before he was due to return with the radio he was killed by a blow from an axe struck by a treacherous sailor. In January 1945, Mrs Marchesi, wife of the

Communist leader Concetto Marchesi, and her daughter Mendelssohn, married to an American Jew, were hidden in my house with the help of Dr Marchesi, Concetto's brother. Concetto had fled to Switzerland to avoid arrest by the fascists. They stayed in my house for 25 days at the same time as the two English officers were also hidden in the house. It was vital that no one know of the presence of the English officers and we were successful. The two Englishmen had remained in my home until 24 January 1945 except for a brief stay in Baiardo.

On 24 January 1945, Dr Marchesi rushed to my house and said that the Germans were to leave within 2 days, taking a number of hostages with them, of which I was at the top of the list. We had to evacuate the villa. Marchesi took his sister-in-law and niece to another location and we took refuge in the empty villa of Kurt Hermann, but without his knowledge. The two English officers were guided at night by my son through the mountains to reach a safe house. My son then returned to the coast to await events. The news of the German retreat turned out to be inaccurate as they remained for a further three months. But the two Englishmen, who were now with the partisans in the mountains and on the coast of Vallecrosia, finally reached France and safety. Today they write from England.

During the stay of the two English officers in our house, a courageous act was undertaken by Dr Ronga, who was called by us to extract a tooth from one of the English officers. He arrived from San Remo without hesitation and carefully safeguarded the information. The two British officers are called:

Michael Ross
George Bell

We had additional help in hiding the two Englishmen from the partisan Luigi Negro, who was the chauffeur at the Villa Hermann at the Madonna della Ruota. We also had the two officers hidden in the villa despite the presence of the Germans in the area and the risk of snap searches by them.

The Dr Marchesi mentioned by Beppe in his account is Salvatore Marchesi, the brother of Concetto Marchesi and a leading partisan commander in the area of Bordighera and San Remo. He was a very good friend of Beppe, and it was he who asked Beppe to shelter his brother's wife, Ada, and her daughter, Lidia Mendelssohn. Much has already been written on Salvatore's important contribution as a partisan by Sergio Favretto.[25] Favretto has also written on Beppe's war effort as well as his bravery in sheltering Michael Ross and George Bell. He has plans to write more on Beppe, whose war contribution he feels has been understated, although much has been written on him as an artist.

Considering the extent of the events during this period, Beppe's account is very brief, factual and unemotional. It is not known when exactly he wrote this account, but for security reasons it is unlikely to have been written before the end of the war. Beppe's daughter, Giovanna, was to marry Michael Ross in October 1946, and there is no mention of this event in Beppe's account. It is therefore likely that the account was written before October 1946.

To whom it was addressed remains a mystery. It seems likely that it was written following a specific request. The account has various corrections and deletions and would appear to be a draft. If so, the whereabouts of any final document is unknown. Perhaps it was requested by the post-war Allied occupation forces or by the partisan organisation to form part of an historical archive?

The manuscript has never before been taken into account by historians. In 2019, however, it was included in an essay by Francesco Mocci in an account he had written of Captain Gino Punzi, a partisan commander also mentioned by Beppe in his account.[26]

What is particularly interesting is the light this manuscript sheds on Beppe's involvement with the partisans. It is clear that his involvement ran far deeper than his family were aware of, as the incidents mentioned by Beppe were not known by his family or by Michael Ross. Beppe had clearly decided not to share his partisan activities with his family or the two British officers he had sheltered, as it would have been extremely dangerous. He realised that, in the event of any of his family being questioned, the lives of many would have been placed in jeopardy.

Beppe's account is very much in keeping with Michael Ross's book *The British Partisan*, but Michael certainly did not have a copy of Beppe's account. Both accounts, however, are understated with regard to the dangers that were faced and risks that were taken by escaped prisoners of war, the partisans and, of course, Beppe, who was risking not only his life but those of his whole family.

---

[25] Sergio Favretto, 'Il fratello e la famiglia di Concetto Marchesi nella resistenza', *Quaderni di Storia 93*, January–June 2021
[26] Francesco Mocci, *Il capitano Gino Punzi* (Pinerolo: Alzani, 2019)

This certificate is awarded to

Porcheddu Giuseppe

as a token of gratitude for and appreciation of the help given to the Sailors, Soldiers and Airmen of the British Commonwealth of Nations, which enabled them to escape from, or evade capture by the enemy.

H.R. Alexander

1939-1945

Field-Marshal,
Supreme Allied Commander,
Mediterranean Theatre

Field Marshal Alexander's letter of thanks to Beppe. Ross Family Archive.

CHAPTER XV

A Return to Painting

The end of the war must have been an incredible relief to Beppe and his family, lifting the huge burden of all the risks he had taken on their lives. He painted throughout the war, which must have been some relief and distraction from his considerable worries.

Beppe became disillusioned with post-war Italian politics as his hope for better government did not materialise. Italy abolished the monarchy, blaming King Victor Emmanuel for his support of Mussolini and for taking Italy into the war alongside Germany. The king abdicated in 1946 and died a year later in Alexandria.

Beppe, however, was now able to concentrate on his paintings and started to organise exhibitions once more. He joined the Group of Venice, a collaboration between a number of like-minded illustrators, which included Hugo Pratt, Giorgio Bellavitis, Mario Faustinelli, Leone Frollo, Sergio Asteriti, Fernando Carcupino, Damiano Damiani and Dino Battaglia. Hugo Pratt, in particular, drew much inspiration from Beppe's art. Together they launched the magazine *Asso di Picche* ('Ace of Spades'), an Italian comic series featuring an eponymous masked crime fighter who combats an international crime syndicate known as the Band of Panthers. The action occurs all over the world, but chiefly in a dark, melancholic version of San Francisco.

One of the many famous people who knew Beppe during this period was Italo Calvino (1923–1985). Calvino was born in Cuba but grew up in San Remo, a short distance from Bordighera. He was Italy's most important post-war novelist. He was also an influential literary critic and a scholarly and entertaining letter-writer. Also fiercely anti-fascist, he and his brother, Floriano, were forced into hiding during the war to avoid being conscripted under Mussolini's Fascist Republic of Salò. They would eventually join the partisans to fight in the Ligurian Alps above their home town of San Remo.

In Calvino's *Into the War*[27] first published in 1954, he describes the Italy of 1940 in a mixture of memory and fiction. He also wrote about his experiences

---

[27] Italo Calvino, *Into the War* (London: Penguin, 2011)

as a partisan fighting the fascists in one of his autobiographical essays in *The Road to San Giovanni*,[28] published by his wife after his death in 1985. The piece is entitled 'Memories of a Battle'. In it, Calvino describes his time in the Figaro battalion of the partisans and a major attack by the partisans on the fascists. His battalion was part of a partisan division commanded by Vitto, and their orders were to gather at dawn around Baiardo. This was the same partisan commander who had interrogated Ross and Bell, having suspected that they were German spies. In Calvino's novel *The Path to the Spiders' Nests*,[29] he modelled his Commandante Ferriera on Vitto.

G Vittorio Guglielmo (Vitto) was born in San Remo, to the east of Bordighera, in 1916. He fought in the International Brigade in the Spanish Civil War and commanded the partisan Garibaldi division in northern Italy. A memorial to him was erected in Loreto, a village in the municipality of Triora in Liguria on the French border. This was an area that would have seen considerable partisan activity.

Baiardo had changed hands a number of times and, at the time of the battle Calvino participated in, was being held by the fascist Bersaglieri brigade. The partisans' attack was fought off, and Calvino describes his part in the encounter and the death of one of his friends. Baiardo was also the place where Ross and Bell had their first encounter with the partisans when they met Renato Brunati.

Calvino was to become an acclaimed novelist. *The Path to the Spiders' Nests* was inspired by his time as a partisan. This was his first novel and was published in 1947 to great acclaim.

In a letter of 8 January 1973 to Antonio Faeti[30] on the subject of the latter's recent book on Italian illustrators, *Guardare le figure*,[31] Calvino mentions Beppe, whom he knew whilst the family lived in Bordighera. He goes on to comment that he knew many people who knew Beppe well. Faeti had featured Beppe in his book as one the great Italian narrative illustrators in the style of the great English illustrators.

In his letter to Faeti, Calvino describes Beppe as 'a very refined, gentlemanly, elegant, and cultured person who professed a Christian-Communist mysticism and he frequented anti-fascist circles before, during and after the Resistance'.

---

[28] Italo Calvino, *The Road to San Giovanni* (London: Penguin, 2009)

[29] Italo Calvino, *The Path to the Spiders' Nests* (London: Penguin, 2009)

[30] Michael Wood, *Italo Calvino: Letters, 1941–1985* (Princeton, NJ: Princeton University Press, 2013, p. 423)

[31] Antonio Faeti, *Guardare le figure* (Rome: Donzelli, 2011, pp. 370–373)

Beppe's daughter, Giovanna, confirmed Beppe's communist sympathies. But the driver in this respect was his concern for the inequality in Italy. He would often help the poor, and his Christian generosity towards anyone who called on the house for food was well known. He also organised his children to take food to local people who had fallen on hard times. It was no coincidence that many of the poor in Italy were also anti-fascist. It was likely that Beppe's privileged upbringing led him to help those less fortunate than himself.

Beppe was to instil his Christian beliefs in his children. Although their upbringing was probably stricter than in other families, his children would always be grateful for their education, ability in languages and undoubted musical talents.

Italo Calvino, partisan and famous author who knew Beppe and wrote about his mysterious disappearance.

There was a daily routine of exercise and gymnastics followed by music practice and education.

Visitors invited to the house included Arturo Benedetti Michelangeli (1920–1995), considered by many to be the greatest classical pianist of the twentieth century. The famous Italian composer and pianist Franco Alfano (1875–1954) was another visitor and family friend. Alfano was famous for completing Puccini's opera *Turandot*. The opera was unfinished when Puccini died in 1924. Alfano based his composition on notes left by Puccini and finished the score in 1926. When Michael Ross married Giovanna, one of the witnesses was Alfano.

Music certainly helped all the family to cope with the harsh and dangerous years of the war. Beppe and his son Bitita played the violin whilst Giovanna played the piano and Ninilla the cello. It was unsurprising that all the children were to become accomplished musicians and Bitita went on to become first violin with the San Remo orchestra. The family's love of music did not go unnoticed during the war, and the German officers in the area considered the family a touch eccentric as they appeared to play music all day.

Beppe was also prepared to encourage art in the young. Indeed, a young Italian girl, Bruna, who also lived in Bordighera, was to become a frequent visitor to the family home for art lessons. This was to lead to some family tensions, as Rita was to suspect that Beppe had become infatuated with the young girl. This was something Beppe denied, but the suspicion remained even amongst his children. Rita, who had always regarded Beppe as a genius who could do no wrong, had started to doubt his intentions.

CHAPTER XVI

Disappearance

On 27 December 1947 something happened which was to change the lives of the Porcheddu family forever. Whilst in Rome arranging an exhibition of his art, Beppe disappeared. He was aged only forty-nine.

His disappearance, perhaps without the significance of that of the famous Italian physicist Ettore Majorana in 1938, was nevertheless just as unfathomable and mysterious. In exploring Beppe's life and works, perhaps clues may be found to explain the extraordinary chain of events that led to his disappearance.

Beppe and Rita's marriage appeared to everyone to be a happy one, which made Beppe's disappearance without explanation even more curious. The twin daughters, Giovanna and Ninilla, were both married on 11 October 1946 in the family villa in Arzilia, having obtained special permission from the Catholic Church. They gave birth to their first children in November and December 1947 in Austria, where their husbands, still in the army, were serving in the occupied country. Beppe and Rita visited their first grandchildren, and Beppe's passport was stamped on entry on 6 November and on leaving Austria on 14 December. He had made the special trip to see his daughters and his grandchildren, which could not have been easy given his disability. Perhaps he was saying a final farewell, unbeknown to the family, as he was to disappear a mere thirteen days later.

After visiting his daughters, Beppe returned alone to Bordighera. He was in the middle of planning an exhibition of his paintings in Rome. Rita remained in Austria, staying with her daughters and first grandchildren.

The day after Beppe's return to Italy he wrote a letter to Rita, dated 16 December 1947.[32] He describes the activities of Marte, the much-loved family dog, a Newfoundland, and details about the house following their absence. He describes his great sense of melancholy and depression and being unable to sleep at night. He mentions having had lunch in a restaurant to 'avoid the voices in the kitchen'. He describes life as being

---

[32] Letter, Beppe Porcheddu to his wife Rita, 16 December 1947

neither interesting nor engaging but says that his focus is on his forthcoming exhibition in Rome. He takes comfort in knowing his daughters are now both happily married with their own families. He is, however, clearly troubled, making comments on self-harm, needing to move if he is to live and being incapable of finding enjoyment and comfort. He comments that it is now a very bad moment for him and hopes for calmer times in the future. He even suggests that Rita should stay longer in Austria with their daughters in order to avoid his melancholy. He is resentful of his wretched mood and the fine weather, and the lightheartedness of others does nothing for him. He ends his letter affectionately towards Rita, wishing her serene days and saying that he will write again soon.

Another letter from Beppe, posted from Bordighera on 18 December to his sister Ambrogia,[33] may have been a cryptic farewell and prelude to his disappearance. In his letter he writes that 'life is a continual betrayal. The most beautiful dreams remain dreams. Who knows when we'll meet again?'

The next day Beppe took the train to Rome and booked into a hotel. He was only in the hotel for two days as an old friend, Piero Giacometti, a well-known Italian author who was organising the exhibition of Beppe's paintings, invited Beppe to come and stay with him. They spent Christmas together, and on 27 December Beppe said he was going out to undertake some business. He was never to be seen again. He left his walking cane, without which he would have been unable to walk far, and also his passport in his room. The passport was current, although it was due to expire on 1 June 1948. In the room was also a letter to Rita.

In 2017 Alessandra Alexandroff, the daughter of Giovanna, interviewed Maci Monti, the ninety-four-year-old daughter of Professor Raffaello Monti.[34] Monti was a very good friend of Beppe and, as described earlier, had moved his family to a chateau in Toulouse to escape fascism as a result of his outspoken opposition. Maci confirmed that Monti had lived there for about ten years and that Beppe and his family moved there in 1936 for the same reasons. They occupied a wing of the chateau and even brought a considerable amount of furniture with them. Maci remembers their time together as an extremely happy one. Beppe was always full of plans and amusements for the children, who all went to French schools. Beppe painted and, of course, the music lessons continued.

---

[33] Letter, Beppe Porcheddu to his sister Ambrogia, 18 December 1947
[34] Interview, Alessandra Alexandroff and Maci Monti, 2017

Maci was extremely lucid, with an excellent memory of Beppe and the circumstances surrounding his mysterious disappearance. She recalled that the disappearance of Beppe was a huge shock to everyone. Beppe and Rita had always had a very happy marriage, and Rita found his disappearance nearly impossible to deal with. She used to go to a tavern in Turin, where they used to meet secretly in the very early days of their friendship, and point to the table where they used to sit. She hoped that one day she would find him just sitting there, waiting for her.

After Beppe returned to Italy alone, having left Rita to extend her time in Austria with her daughters and the two grandchildren, Maci saw him in the market square in Bordighera. He waved across to her, saying that he would shortly be leaving for Rome but would come and see her father on his return. He seemed totally normal and there was no hint that he was soon to disappear.

Maci confirmed that the search for Beppe was very thorough. Even the length of the Tiber was searched, particularly its estuary at the sea, and account was taken of tidal movements, but all to no avail.

Rita then made a surprise visit to Padre Pio (1887–1968), the Capuchin friar, stigmatist and mystic who was to be canonised in 2002 by Pope John Paul II. Maci explained that the reason Rita visited Padre Pio was because she discovered that Beppe had gone to visit him some months before. Maci knew this as her father had accompanied Beppe.

Beppe must have revealed something to Padre Pio, despite his previous stance that he would not confess to a mere mortal on Earth. Padre Pio gave him a penance which was to last the unusually long time of six months, ending in December 1947, the month in which he was to disappear. The reason for the imposition of this penance is not known, but clearly it had to be related to a major sin confessed to Padre Pio.

When Rita met Padre Pio he said not to look for Beppe. He said he thought Beppe was still alive and would one day return. It was for this reason that Rita did not give up hope for many years that her beloved Beppe would return.

Maci also commented on the letter that Beppe had written to Rita, which had been left in the room in Rome after his disappearance. Rita could not comprehend the contents of Beppe's letter; she was probably in shock. She and her son Bitita had rushed round to Monti's house and they read the letter together, trying to make sense of it all. Bitita, in particular, was devastated. The letter was like a lightning bolt. Maci remembers that in the letter, Beppe told Rita that she was strong, that he was leaving and that she was not to look for him. He said his daughters were now married and well settled and that Bitita was now no longer a boy. This was hardly an explanation and must have made it all the more difficult for the family.

Maci also recalls that, although Beppe had left various documents in his room in Rome, he took his leg brace, a result of his World War I wounds, with him. He could not have walked far without it.

Alessandra raised the rumour of 'another woman' with Maci. This was the girl called Bruna mentioned earlier. Maci had not raised this herself and probably thought that the story had been buried a long time ago. She immediately said that 'the girl' was the whole problem and that Beppe had fallen in love with her. Maci added that Bruna was from Ventimiglia and she did not think that she had run away with Beppe as she thought Bruna had continued to live in Ventimiglia after his disappearance.

Maci mentioned the family's theory that Beppe was now living anonymously in a monastery. There was one located near Rome which had produced leaflets with drawings on them in a style similar to Beppe's. Porcheddu family friends visited the monastery to ask about Beppe, but the monks denied having seen him. It was well known, however, that monasteries took in people, especially those suffering from a spiritual crisis, and would never reveal a name without the permission of the individual in question. Perhaps Beppe had sought refuge in a monastery, where the vow of silence and the unquestioning acceptance of a refugee provided him with protection and isolation from an unhappy world? The family were to cling to this theory. It may have suited them emotionally and even given some comfort. Perhaps one day he would return to Bordighera and continue his family life and painting as if nothing had happened.

It was to be many years before the family gave up hope. Perhaps Rita never gave up hope.

Maci concluded her account by saying that Beppe's disappearance was a tragedy which touched many people.

Italo Calvino was to note later[35] that people still continued to talk of Beppe's mysterious disappearance many years after the event. He went on to surmise that 'the only explanation one can come up with is that this was a Buddhist-type religious crisis which finally led to his total loss of self'.

Mario Faustinelli, in his introduction to the 1978 reprint of *Il castello di San Velario*,[36] comments on Beppe's disappearance and says that it would have been nearly impossible, wherever he fled to, for Beppe to have been

---

[35] Michael Wood, *Italo Calvino: Letters, 1941–1985* (Princeton, NJ: Princeton University Press, 2013, p. 423)
[36] Beppe Porcheddu, *Il castello di San Velario* (Milan: Editoriali d'Ami, 1978)

able to start another life under an assumed name and still paint. His art, if it appeared in public, would have been immediately recognised as it was unique in style, no matter how his paintings might have been signed.

One has to ask how many people, if any, really knew and understood Beppe. Could Italo Calvino have been close to the truth when he remarked that Beppe had perhaps lost his sense of self? The risks he took in his anti-fascist stance, both for himself and for his family, must have been an intolerable burden on the man. Because of the dangers these were crosses he had to bear himself and could not be shared. Did this burden, once he saw both his daughters happily married with their own families, become so intolerable that solace would only be found in his disappearance and perhaps the taking of his own life?

With medical advances in the recognition of forms of mental illness or anxiety disorders, the condition of post-traumatic stress disorder (PTSD) has been identified in war veterans as well as those who have experienced or witnessed harrowing events. It can develop immediately after someone experiences a disturbing event, or it can occur weeks, months or even years later. Cases of PTSD were first documented during World War I when soldiers developed shell shock as a result of the harrowing conditions in the trenches. It was not officially recognised as a mental health condition until 1980, when it was included in the *Diagnostic and Statistical Manual of Mental Disorders*, developed by the American Psychiatric Association.

In the case of Beppe, all the preconditions for PTSD were clearly present: the horrors of trench warfare in the First World War in the most harsh conditions in the Austro-Italian mountains, his near-death from injuries from a grenade, his permanent disability with a leg which was nearly amputated, his persistent anti-fascist stance leading to arrest and interrogation, work in support of the partisans, the torture and execution of one of his best friends, the sheltering of British escaped prisoners of war and the consequent risk to himself and his entire family. Whilst there is no corroborating medical evidence that Beppe was suffering from PTSD, it is difficult to imagine a more likely sufferer, given his past experiences and his disappearance in late 1947.

Inevitably, through his anti-fascism, Beppe had made many enemies. The post-war period saw many scores being settled, and there is the possibility that Beppe's disappearance may have been linked to his political activities. One can but imagine how difficult it must have been for Rita and his children not to have even a hint of an explanation. All Rita was left with was a letter from Beppe asking that no one should look for him.

CHAPTER XVII

Beppe the Enigma

Interest in Beppe's strange disappearance increased over the years, focusing on the man's complex and perhaps troubled personality. Were any clues to be found in his art? His art was complex, a mixture of religious themes, the romantic, the allegoric and the underworld, often combined in the same painting. The images are often stark, even brutal, so much so that some disturbed his young family.

Beppe was a man of undoubted moral principles, religious but with contradictions as he could not adhere to all the tenets of his Catholic faith. He could not bring himself to attend confession, which was obligatory if sins were to be forgiven. His explanation was that he would not confess to any mortal, despite the Catholic tenet that the priest in the confessional box represented God on Earth. Instead, he said he confessed directly to God. Was his refusal to confess to a priest some pick-and-mix attitude to the teachings of the Catholic Church or a reflection of the very private nature of the man, perhaps with many secrets?

Final clues were found in the Porcheddu family papers many years after Beppe's disappearance. They were contained in a small black writing book and consisted of various letters written by Beppe to his son Bitita, letters from Giovanni Turin to Beppe, to Bitita and to Rita, and finally a folded typed postscript which could only have been written by Beppe. The postscript was the last known piece of writing by Beppe.

Giovanni Turin was a close friend from the family's days in Turin. He was a professor of history and philosophy and, like Beppe, a staunch anti-fascist, so much so that he also had to leave Italy and emigrated to Tucumán in Argentina in 1939. He wrote several books whilst a professor at the University of Tucumán. He sent a copy of one of his books to Beppe, *Socrates, Galileo, Leopardi*, published in 1947, with an inscription from Buenos Aries, dated 4 November 1948. He writes to his dear friend Beppe that he is not yet dead. Beppe never received the book as he had already disappeared. The book has now been given to Mark Turin, Giovanni's grandson, an acclaimed academic now living in Canada.

In a further letter dated 4 September 1949,[37] Giovanni refers to not answering Beppe's last letter to him. It is not known when Beppe wrote this letter, but it is clear that Giovanni was unaware that Beppe had disappeared in December 1947. Giovanni adds that he had not wanted to reply as he himself had been in as difficult a position as Beppe.

Clearly, Beppe had confessed something to Giovanni, and Giovanni hints at sharing some private drama. In the case of Beppe this might have been an infatuation with the younger woman, Bruna. Sadly, little remains of Giovanni's papers or letters as his wife, Elda, burnt them all on his death.

The letter to Beppe must have been opened by the Porcheddu family, as Giovanni subsequently wrote a letter to Rita dated 14 July 1950 and was now aware that Beppe had disappeared. He referred to a private letter that he had written previously to Beppe in which he confessed to 'terrible things'. His son, Duccio, was to hand-deliver the letter to Beppe. The whereabouts of this letter to Beppe are unknown, but it is possible that it was destroyed. In his letter to Rita Giovanni says that he wishes to come back to Italy to assist in the search for Beppe but sheds no light on why Beppe may have disappeared.

The key remaining piece of evidence concerning the disappearance of Beppe is the typed postscript which was also in the black exercise book. It was clearly the last page of a letter, but the letter itself is missing. It was typed on very thin sheet, the type used for airmail letters.

A translation of the postscript follows:

PS. I forget that I owe a painting to a teacher of my son. I ask you therefore to set aside the one with Orpheus and Eurydice, the three infernal rages and the hunting dog; it is easily recognisable. In your own time you can post it, recorded and non-urgent and signed by you as if written by Rita. Sorry, thanks. Send to Bordighera or to Torino [Turin]. *It would be hard if public curiosity and circumstances do not succeed in tracking me down. But if that happens,* [I feel sure that] *no one will recognise me – except perhaps you. I beg you not to acknowledge me – in fact, not to know me from this point on. To everyone it must look like I have gone on a long voyage. Thank you!*

In the same way, I beg you to let it be that the only people who know the reality of my journey are Rita and Bruna – it will be [to all intents and purposes] *a disappearance.*

---

[37] Letter, Giovanni Turin to Beppe Porcheddu, 4 September 1949

Bruna is healthy and intact! I have respected her.
The suitcases are open. Please close them yourself with the keys on the side table. The chest closes with a padlock.

The most likely recipient of this letter would have been Piero Giacometti, the Italian author and friend with whom Beppe had been staying. The wording indicates that it was left in his room for Giacometti to find after Beppe had disappeared – hence the tying up of various loose ends and the request to close the suitcases. Not all Beppe's instructions were carried out, as the painting referred to is still in the Porcheddu family's collection.

Although there is no date attached to the postscript, it may, along with the enigmatic (farewell?) letter he wrote to his sister from Bordighera just before he disappeared, have been one of the last letters Beppe wrote. The fact that he writes that only Rita and Bruna should know of his 'real' journey indicates that there were three letters and the other two were for Rita and Bruna. It is interesting to note that this letter is typed, whilst the remainder of Beppe's correspondence in November and December was in manuscript.

The reference to Bruna is very interesting. The frequency of her lessons with Beppe had aroused the family's suspicions that a relationship between the two was developing. Rita became very depressed, so much so that one of the daughters, Giovanna, wrote to her father expressing her disappointment with his behaviour. Giovanna in her letter writes that she had seen her father always on a pedestal but had now realised he had 'feet of clay'.

It is clear from this postscript that Beppe denied that there had been an inappropriate relationship, although clearly he had become close to Bruna. As previously mentioned, nothing more of significance was heard of Bruna. From the wording of the postscript there is no hint that Bruna joined Beppe following his disappearance.

*

The Porcheddu family was extremely well known in Italy, and Beppe's disappearance received considerable press coverage. Beppe's brother-in-law Giorgio Bardanzellu, who was now a prominent member of the Italian parliament, ensured that no stone was left unturned in the search for Beppe. Over the decades many have investigated his disappearance, but no one has ever found an explanation. It was several years after his disappearance that Beppe was finally certified as dead and a war widow's pension awarded to Rita, which was to become an important source of income to her in her later years.

Rita died in Bordighera on 19 March 1987, still not knowing the reason for her husband's disappearance nor what had become of him. One can only imagine what a heavy cross it must have been for her to bear.

Rita was buried in the Porcheddu family tomb in Turin, designed by Edoardo Rubino. Rubino was a famous Italian sculptor, born in Turin in 1871, and knew Beppe's father, Giovanni, well. When Giovanni's wife, Amalia, died very young in 1912, Giovanni commissioned Rubino to build a monumental tomb in the Turin Cemetery, now known as 'Il Cimitero Monumentale di Torino' in recognition of the many famous sculptures and monuments erected there. Few wealthy middle-class Italians of the nineteenth century were art collectors, instead spending their money on funerary sculpture by building ornate and often beautiful monuments to deceased members of their families.

The tomb's architect was Giulio Casanova, who was born in Minerbio in 1875 and died in Bologna in 1961. His many projects in Italy included the design for the shrine for the Holy Shroud in Turin Cathedral in 1931.

The Porcheddu tomb was to become one of Rubino's most famous works and is visited regularly by students of sculpture and architecture. Rubino died in Turin in 1954.

Porcheddu family tomb, Turin. Designed by the famous Italian sculptor Edoardo Rubino.

CHAPTER XVIII

An Artistic Legacy

To mark the sixtieth anniversary of the disappearance of Beppe Porcheddu, a major retrospective exhibition of many of his paintings, illustrations and ceramics was held in Turin from 25 October to 24 November 2007 at the Galleria D'Arte Narciso. Many members of the family attended. The exhibition proved highly popular and celebrated once again Beppe's extraordinary life and works.

The legacy of Beppe clearly lives on and his art is much sought after, particularly in Italy. His use of the medium of watercolour on maple wood, incorporating the grain, was particularly distinctive of his style. Altogether, Beppe illustrated more than fifty volumes and designed displays, advertisements, engravings, boxes for chocolates, toys, furniture and even fabrics in his inimitable style.

In his 1928 introduction to *Disegni di Giuseppe Porcheddu*,[38] Leonardo Bistolfi writes initially on the art of a seven-year-old Beppe, an

Sagittarius, Virgo and Aquarius by Beppe, 1942, watercolour on maple.

---

[38] Leonardo Bistolfi, *Disegni di Giuseppe Porcheddu* (Turin, 1928)

Constellations by Beppe, 1942, watercolour on maple..

extraordinary child prodigy; of his fantastic landscapes, strange groups of human bodies, scenes of fairy tales from a hand skilled enough to give relief to the several stages undergone by shape and space. Bistolfi asked Beppe's father how his son had managed to copy all those images, to which his father replied that they were all entirely original paintings.

Over the next few years Bistolfi made frequent visits to Beppe's family home in Turin. He took a great interest in observing Beppe's developing artistic talent and in particular how he used emotion, imagination and allegory in his paintings and drawings. Bistolfi noted that few other artists had Beppe's talent for literary illustration, which at first sight was caricature in form, with those depicted appearing as if they were actually speaking. His art seemed to speak through his paintbrush. Bistolfi felt that it seemed as if Beppe had already lived all those lives and tales and they were now on paper.

One of Beppe's particular strengths was his ability to reflect the past, often delving deep into history, bringing it to life. Beppe's art was instinctive; he had no need for references or human models. He already had the images in his mind through his extraordinary imagination.

Over time, Beppe's art became more expressive and vigorous. Writers would merely suggest a subject and Beppe was able to develop it as if he were a musician, finding the best way of bringing the subject to life, transforming images into reality. His personality would vanish in the process and he would borrow one suited to the character of the theme that he was developing. Such perfect blending of the poet's vision with the painter's fulfilment was, according to Bistolfi, one of Beppe's finest gifts. His drawings never fail to reveal a long and patient study of the story they are meant to depict. But, more than that, they bring the story to life, giving it light, shape and sensations for the reader. Beppe had a perception that seemed to reflect the writer's inner thoughts. Bistolfi concludes his appreciation of Beppe by emphasising the spiritual dimension of his art and the ability and passion to stretch the boundaries of his artistic genius continually.

Beppe also exhibited a natural inclination for what Massimo Oldoni calls 'the perfect combination of symbols of a medieval world, which is expressed by metaphors like no other previous civilization'. Oldoni's 2008 book *Gerberto e il suo fantasma*[39] identifies in Beppe's paintings the use of the fortress, the abbey, the forest and the horseman, soldiers in armour and riding elegant but muscular horses, which appear in many of his paintings and illustrations. His iconic St George and the Dragon, which regularly appeared in designs for bookplates, invitations and greeting cards, reflected Beppe's passion for the medieval world and fantasies.

In 1972 Antonio Faeti published his acclaimed book *Guardare le figure*.[40] In it he devotes several pages to Beppe. He placed Beppe in a rare group of painters who were able to illustrate storytelling so effectively. He

Allegory of Life by Beppe, 1943, watercolour on maple.

---

[39] Massimo Oldoni, *Gerberto e il suo fantasma* (Naples: Liguori, 2008)
[40] Antonio Faeti, *Guardare le figure* (Rome: Donzelli, 2011, pp. 370–373)

Orpheus and Eurydice by Beppe, 1942, watercolour on maple.

commented that Beppe did not differ greatly in a technical way from the well-known English illustrators. Beppe replicated the grotesque in terms of graphic expression. His figures constantly avoided the conventional and were always beyond the obvious and normal. It was as if he wanted to paint outside the credible, looking beyond stereotypes, forcing Beppe towards deformity in his characters as if inhabiting the underworld.

Amongst the numerous works by Beppe, one in particular demonstrates his wish to seek refuge from the definitive world. In fact, Beppe retreats from history, distorts the real and resides only in his own world. This work,

The Song of Frescobaldi by Beppe, 1942, watercolour on maple.

Fifteenth-century Allegory by Beppe, 1942, watercolour on maple. Ross Family Collection.

Il castello di San Velario e il mistero degli specchi velati, is in two parts and is a long graphic novel first edited and published by Mondadori in 1948. It is fully representative of the man, as if the subject were Beppe himself, who never leaves the confines of his own world. He condenses his graphic designs to those full of shade and movement, oscillating between images of the grotesque. In this story the threads of Beppe's world are intertwined: the maritime, adventures, fables and the darker novel. The plot leaves the reader with the sense of an ambiguous tale with a number of differing and complex threads.

Gulliver's Travels, illustrated by Beppe. Unpublished, but the original plates were stolen and then rediscovered. Some plates auctioned in May 2019.

Il castello di San Velario, written and illustrated by Beppe, was republished by Editoriali d'Ami in 1978. Mario Faustinelli, in his introduction,[41] describes Beppe as one of the greatest Italian painters of his generation and yet probably little known.

Piemonte di carta: la tradizione piemontese del fumetto, published by Edizione d'Arte Lo Scarabeo in 1995,[42] has a chapter devoted to Beppe in an appreciation by Gianni Milone, a well-known illustrator himself. Milone covers Beppe's main works and publications, emphasising the influence of English illustrators, such as Arthur Rackham, on the young boy and man. The chapter includes illustrations from *I viaggi di Gulliver*, which was scheduled to be published by Mondadori in *Topolino*. Sadly the publishing house was closed and so the sixty double pages of illustrations were never formally published. Unfortunately, they were subsequently stolen at Milan station whilst being transported in a suitcase by an acquaintance of the family. Those who had viewed the illustrations at the time were unanimous as to their originality and quality. In an earlier publication by Milone, *Come disegnare*, he uses the *Gulliver* illustrations to demonstrate Beppe's skill and storytelling. Milone concludes that Beppe's disappearance in late 1947 robbed Italy of one of its greatest illustrators of the era.

This, however, was not the end of the story of the *Gulliver* drawings. In an article, published on 9 May 2019, on lost works of illustrative art, the auction house of Urania Casa d'Aste announced that twenty-five original plates of Beppe's *Gulliver* would be auctioned on 11 May.[43] The article describes Beppe as one of the most important Italian illustrators of the first half of the twentieth century, responsible for many volumes from the most famous publishing houses in Italy such as Lattes, De Agostini and Teves. It mentions that his masterpiece was considered *The*

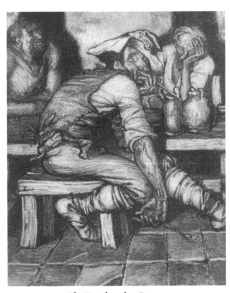

The Drinkers by Beppe.

[41] Beppe Porcheddu, *Il castello di San Velario* (Milan: Editoriali d'Ami, 1978)

[42] Gianni Milone, *Piemonte di carta* (Turin: Edizioni d'Arte Lo Scarabeo, 1995)

[43] 'Ritrovato il Gulliver di Porcheddu, capolavoro perduto del fumetto italiano', *Fumettologica*, 9 May 2019

Adventures of Pinocchio, published by Paravia in 1942, illustrated on light grey or beige paper in three different shades of brick red, blue and white. The original drawings were fortuitously saved when the publishing house was destroyed by Allied bombing in World War II.

Beppe's work on *Gulliver* had previously slowed down and then ceased, possibly because of a change of director at the publishing house or new priorities. Since then, of course, Beppe had disappeared. His work on *Gulliver* had become a mystery. Some even doubted that it had existed. Rita, however, had kept all his preparatory drawings, and we now know that the complete works consisted of sixty double plates. The print-ready originals, as mentioned, were later to disappear.

In 1988 Disney Italy took over the publication of Disney's comic books in Italy, after over fifty years of management by Mondadori. The new company decided to clear a warehouse on the outskirts of Milan and to dispose of newspapers, printing proofs and other documents. Somehow much of the material destined for recycling was saved. The large original plates of Beppe's *Gulliver* illustrations (62.5 x 42.5 cm) were probably amongst the saved material and reappeared a few years ago in the shop of an antique dealer in Grosseto. Of the original sixty double plates twenty-five had been saved. The Urania sales catalogue reproduced the plates for the first time and clearly demonstrated Beppe's skill and artistic talent.

In 2007 Enrica Crivello, a postgraduate student at the University of Turin, completed a dissertation on Beppe Porcheddu entitled 'Giuseppe

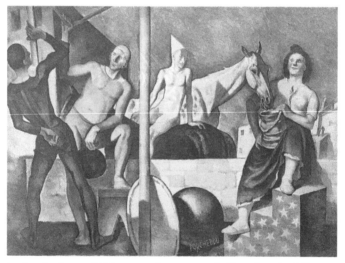

Acrobats by Beppe, 1943, watercolour on maple. Ross Family Collection.

Porcheddu, children's illustrator, and decorative art in Turin in the second decade of the twentieth century'.[44] Crivello gives a brief biography of Beppe, repeating much of what had already been recorded in various articles and accounts. Her dissertation is divided into three parts: firstly, how Beppe's experiences influenced his art; secondly, his work as an illustrator and in particular his undoubted talent for bringing children's stories to light, and finally his decorative art, in particular his successful partnership with Lenci and the creation of many charming ceramic pieces. The dissertation also includes her analysis of how Beppe's style as an illustrator evolved and changed between the 1920s and 1940s. Much of her research was made possible by access to the archive at the Foundation Tancredi di Barolo, which is located in the Museum of the School and Children's Books in Turin.

Crivello's observations on Beppe's style of painting are interesting. The dissertation covers the period when Beppe had a particularly successful career as an illustrator of children's books. He was much in demand, as evidenced by the many popular and successful authors who invited Beppe's participation.

Her dissertation does not cover Beppe's early years, nor his last decade of painting, when his anti-fascist views led directly to a reduction in commissions. This latter period is marked by the production of his greatest paintings, all executed with the uncommon technique of watercolour on

The Nativity by Beppe, 1944, watercolour on maple. Ross Family Collection.

[44] Enrica Crivello, 'Giuseppe Porcheddu illustatore per l'infanzia e le arti decorative a Torino nel secondo decennio del novecento' (dissertation, University of Turin, 2007)

wood, with subject matter ranging from biblical scenes such as the resurrection of Lazarus to the allegoric and mythological. Whilst he could clearly illustrate to match the story and the age of the reader, and thus he was capable of changing his style accordingly, his true genius as a painter is best exemplified by his later works.

As mentioned, Beppe was heavily influenced by Arthur Rackham, one of the great English illustrators. Many of Rackham's illustrations in the books of Edgar Allen Poe, JM Barrie, Lewis Carroll, Jonathan Swift, Aesop, the Brothers Grimm, Hans Christian Andersen and Oliver Goldsmith inspired Beppe. He acquired an extensive collection of books illustrated by Rackham. In Beppe's art one therefore often sees deformity and death depicted.

Medieval influences are also often present in Beppe's work, as well as the grotesque and macabre. Recurring features are the various ages of man interspersed with Roman and Greek mythology and fantasy. Often the focus included figures of sirens, lizards, the god Dionysus, and sharp hooked noses and malignant expressions perhaps influenced by the 'trend of deformed Nordic ancestry', as written by Eros Belloni in his book *Corridor of Mirrors Veiled*, in which he describes Beppe's art.

The Angel and the Doll by Beppe, 1947, watercolour on maple. Painted as a present for the author by Beppe and presented shortly before Beppe disappeared. Ross Family Collection.

These observations on Beppe's art are intriguing. Could it be that perhaps his tortured soul manifested itself in his art? Perhaps his admitted dark moods, sadness and melancholy in the final days before he disappeared were a final reflection on the man who could no longer cope with life.

On 27 February 2013, Italian television (RAI) broadcasted a documentary on Beppe,[45] and the central feature was an interview with his daughters, Giovanna and Ninilla. They talked about his anti-fascism, his value for freedom of expression and his disappearance. Speculation on his disappearance will undoubtedly continue. His paintings, storytelling and artistic genius, however, live on in the rich legacy he has left for future generations.

So ends the extraordinary tale of Beppe Porcheddu, volunteer soldier in World War I, acclaimed artist, anti-fascist and helper of British escaped prisoners of war in World War II. Ross, Day and Bell would forever be grateful for the risks that many Italians took, and in particular Beppe Porcheddu.

In his war memoir, Ross said that what he had written on Beppe fell far short of the worthy tribute due to this great man. A man who upheld the principles he believed in, come what may, and who, in his own way, contributed much to the Allied cause and to the resistance against fascism.

Interview with Vincenzo Gismondi

Vincenzo Gismondi in his garden in Bordighera with author's son, Jonathan Ross, in August 2003. Vincenzo described the war years and his time with Michael Ross, followed by a trip up into the mountains to show Jonathan the hideouts used by the partisans and hidden tracks.

---

[45] TG3 Liguria for RAI, interview of the two Porcheddu daughters by Michaela Bellenzier, 27 February 2013

Sezione di Bordighera

Bordighera, 12 Ottobre 2015

Gentilissime Signore **Ninilla** e **Giovanna Porcheddu,**

nella ricorrenza del 70° Anniversario della Liberazione dell' Italia dal nazifascismo, l'
Associazione Nazionale dei Partigiani d'Italia, interpretando i sentimenti di tutti cittadini,
desidera ricordare con gratitudine chi si impegnò, con gravissimi rischi e spesso pagando
con la vita, nella Resistenza per restituire pace e libertà al nostro Paese.
Dai libri di storia, le narrazioni e le testimonianze emerge in tutta evidenza il contributo dato
a questo fine dalla Famiglia Porcheddu: da Vostro Padre Giuseppe (Beppe) ai Vostri
rispettivi Mariti. L' ANPI, nel ricordare e darne pubblica testimonianza, vuole esprimerVi un
sentito riconoscente ringraziamento consegnandoVi – se ben accetta– la tessera ANPI *ad
honorem*.
In attesa di conoscere la Vostra opinione su questa iniziativa e a disposizione, anche
personalmente, per eventuali ulteriori delucidazioni, ringraziamo e porgiamo i più cordiali
saluti.

Il Presidente dell' Anpi di Bordighera
(Giorgio Loreti)

PS. Telefono: 348 7067688

Partisan letter of commendation to the Porcheddu family. Presented to Beppe's twin
daughters in October 2015 in recognition of the partisan activities of their father and also of
the contributions made by the daughters' husbands to the Allied cause.

Author and family in 1996 in Pen Bryn, Brecon, when he was commanding 160 (Wales) Brigade.
The occasion was Michael and Giovanna's fiftieth wedding anniversary.
Ross Family Archive.

Bibliography

Belloni, Eros. *Beppe Porcheddu: Castle S. Velario*. Milan: Mondadori, 1948

Bistolfi, Leonardo. *Disegni di Giuseppe Porcheddu*. Turin, 1928

Bizzaro, Leonardo. 'Porcheddu, la matita che spari a natale'. La Repubblica, 20 October 2007

Calvino, Italo. *Into the War*. London: Penguin, 2011

Calvino, Italo. *The Path to the Spiders' Nests*. London: Penguin, 2009

Calvino, Italo. *The Road to San Giovanni*. London: Penguin, 2009.

Cirio, CDE. *Fiabe illustrate da Giuseppe Porcheddu*. San Giovanni a Teduccio, Societa Generale delle Conserve Alimentari Cirio, s.d.

Colombini, Graziella (ed.). *Quando fischiava il vento 1943–1945*. Pinerolo: Alzani, 2015

Crivello, Enrica. 'Giuseppe Porcheddu illustratore per l'infanzia'. Dissertation, University of Turin, 2007

Faeti, Antonio. *Guardare le figure*. Rome: Donzelli, 2011

Galli, Rich. 'Monte Grappa: Italy's Thermopylae'. Great War Society. Retrieved from worldwar1.com/heritage/mtg1.htm

Gilmour, David. *The Pursuit of Italy*. London: Penguin, 2012

Graham, Dominick. *The Escapes and Evasions of an Obstinate Bastard*. Windsor: Wilton65, 2000

Hastings, Max. *All Hell Let Loose*. London: Harper Press, 2011

Kendall, Richard (ed.). *Monet by Himself*. Guild, 1989

MacGalloway, Niall. 'All the king's men? British official policy towards the Italian resistance'. *Retrospectives: A Postgraduate History Journal 2*. University of Warwick, 2013, p. 50

Nelva, Riccardo, and Bruno Signorelli. *Avvento ed evoluzione del calcestruzzo armato in Italia: il sistema Hennebique*. Milan: AITEC, 1990

Oldoni, Massimo. *Gerberto e il suo fantasma: techiche della fantasia e della letteratura nel Medioevo*. Naples: Liguori, 2008

Porcheddu, Beppe. *Il castello di San Velario*. Milan: Editoriali d'Ami, 1978

Rommel, Erwin. *Infantry Attacks*. Barnsley: Frontline, 2019

Ross, Michael. *From Liguria with Love*. London: Minerva Press, 1997. Republished as *The British Partisan*, Barnsley: Pen & Sword, 2019

Ruffino, Giovanni. *Doctor Antonio*. Life Sign Press, 2011

Thompson, Mark. *The White War*. London: Faber, 2008

Tudor, Malcolm. *Beyond the Wire*. Newtown: Emilia, 2009

Vigna, Bepi. 'Grafici e illustratori sardi nella prima metà del Novecento'. icoNUR. Retrieved from iconur.it/storia-delle-immagini/48-grafici-e-illustratori-sardi-nella-prima-meta-del-novecento

Wilks, John and Eileen. *The British Army in Italy, 1917–1918*, Barnsley: Pen & Sword, 2013.

Wood, Michael. *Italo Calvino: Letters, 1941–1985*, Princeton, NJ: Princeton University Press, 2013.

APPENDIX I

Books and Publications Illustrated by Beppe Porcheddu

Bedier, Joseph. *Il romanzo di Tristano e Isotta* (The Romance of Tristan and Isolde). Milan: De Agostini, 1929

Bersanetti, Alda. *Avventura nella Russia Bolscevica* (Adventure in Bolshevik Russia). Turin: SEI, 1942

Bistolfi, Gian. *Racconti così* (Stories So). Milan: Garzanti, 1944

Bistolfi, Gian. *Un po di destino* (A Little Fate). Turin: Alberto Giani, 1927

Bruno, E. *Passeggiate storiche Torinesi* (Scenic Turin). Turin: Frassinelli, 1939

Bulwer-Lytton, Edward. *Gli ultimi giorni di Pompei* (The Last Days of Pompeii). Turin: SEI, 1934

Cipolla, Arnaldo. *Balilla regale* (Royal Table). Milan: Est, 1935

Cipolla, Arnaldo. *Il cuore dei continenti* (The Heart of the Continents). Milan: Mondadori, 1926

Cirio, CDE. *Fiabe illustrate da Giuseppe Porcheddu* (Fables Illustrated by Giuseppe Porcheddu). San Giovanni a Teduccio, Societa Generale delle Conserve Alimentari Cirio, s.d.

Collodi, Carlo. *Le avventure di Pinocchio: storia di un burattino* (The Adventures of Pinocchio: Story of a Puppet). Turin: Paravia, 1942

Cooper, James Fenimore. *Il bravo di Venezia* (The Bravo of Venice). Turin: SEI, 1948

Daudet, Alphonse. *Tartarino di Tarascona*. Milan: De Agostini, 1928

De La Barca, Demon. *I signori dell'infinito* (The Lords of the Infinite). Turin: Paravia, 1923

Diorama. *Il fanciullo che vola* (The Child Who Flies). Milan: Vallardi, 1933

Flaubert, Gustave. *La tentazioni di Sant'Antonio* (The Temptation of St Anthony). Turin: Ramella, 1946

Ghiron, Ugo. *I piccoli canti: poesie per fanciulli* (Small Songs: Poems for

Children). Turin: Paravia, 1921

Jandolo, A. *Torri del Lazio* (Towers of Lazio). Milan: Ceschina, 1941

Luigi, Ugolino. *Guerrino di Castelmaus.* Como: Noseda, 1945

Magri, Rosario. *La bella addormentata* (Sleeping Beauty). Turin: SEI, 1951

Merimee, Prosper. *Colomba* (Dove). Milan: De Agostini, 1928

Michele, Michel. *Ragazzo celebre* (Famous Boy). Como: Noseda, 1945

Nievo, Ippolito. *Angelo di bonta* (Angel of Goodness). Milan: De Agostini, 1929

Osta, Eva. *Filastrocca* (Nursery Rhyme). Turin: Editrice Libraria Italiana, 1938

Osta, Eva. *La storia dei dieci leprottini* (The Story of the Ten Leverets). Trieste: La Editoriale Libraria, s.d.

Porcheddu, Beppe. *Il castello di San Velario* (The Castle of St Velario). *Albo d'Oro 115*. Milan: Mondadori, 1948.

Porcheddu, Beppe, *Il mistero degli specchi velati* (The Mystery of the Veiled Mirrors). *Albo d'Oro 117*. Milan: Mondadori, 1948

Porcheddu, Beppe. *Attestato di merito schola elementare disegno di Beppe Porcheddu* (Elementary School Certificate of Merit). Edizioni d'Arte Porcheddu, 1931

Porcheddu, Beppe. *Veicoli Fiat* (Fiat Vehicles). Turin: Ufficio Stampa Fiat, 1937

Raimondo, Gigi. *Le visioni di Accipiccio* (Visions of Accipiccio). Turin: Paravia, 1921

Raspe, Rudolf Erich. *Le avventure del Barone di Munchausen* (The Adventures of Baron Munchausen). Turin: Paravia, 1934

Rostagni, Augustus. *Romanita perenne: antología latina per la scuola medica* (The Roman Perennial: Latin Anthology for the Medical School). Milan: Mondadori, 1941

Salgari, Emilio. *I ribelli della montagna* (The Mountain Rebels). Turin: Paravia, 1941

Salgari, Emilio. *L'indiana dei monti neri* (The Indian of the Black Mountains). Turin: Paravia, 1943

Tolstoy, Leo. *La felicita domestica* (The Domestic Happiness). Milan: De Agostini, 1928

Wells, EG. *La sirena* (The Mermaid). Milan: De Agostini, 1929

Zucca, Giuseppe. *Sentieri sotto le stelle vol. I: vento nella boscaglia* (Paths Under the Stars vol. I: Woodland Wind). Turin: SEI, 1940

Zucca, Giuseppe. *Sentieri sotto le stelle vol. II: il principe della favola* (Paths Under the Stars vol. II: The Prince of the Fable). Turin: SEI, 1941

Zucca, Giuseppe. *Sentieri sotto le stelle vol. III: sostano le carovane* (Paths Under the Stars vol. III: The Caravan Stop). Turin: SEI, 1941

Illustrations and paintings by Beppe Porcheddu also appear in many other publications listing modern Italian artists and illustrators.

The Medals Awarded to Beppe Porcheddu

CAP. CAV. GUISEPPE PORCHEDDU 3ª ALPINI
1898 – 1947

Ordine della Corona d'Italia (Order of the Crown of Italy)

Beppe was knighted by King Victor Emmanuel III on 18 January 1925 for his contribution to the arts in Italy. He therefore followed his father, who had been knighted by the king for services to construction.

The Order was instituted on 20 February 1868 by King Victor Emmanuel II after the annexation of the Venetian region and the completion of the unification of Italy. It was awarded to Italian and foreign citizens, both civilians and soldiers, as a token of national gratitude for their accomplishments, which could include a long military career. It was divided into five classes: Knight, Officer, Commander, Grand Officer and Grand Cross.

Between the cross arms were four knots of Savoy (love knots) in gold. On the obverse side of the cross was an iron crown encircled in gold and blue; on the reverse there was a black eagle with the arms of Savoy encircled in red.

The Order was named after the famous Iron Crown of Lombardy, kept in Monza's Cathedral and allegedly crafted from a nail of the Holy Cross. The crown was used for the coronations, among many others, of Charlemagne, Napoleon I and all the kings of Italy. Following the fall of the monarchy after World War II the Order was discontinued. It was replaced in 1951 by the Ordine al Merito della Repubblica Italiana ('Meritorious Order of the Republic of Italy').

Croce al Merito di Guerra (War Merit Cross)

Awarded to members of the armed forces for war merit in operations on land, on sea or in the air, after minimum of one year of service in the trenches or elsewhere, in contact with an enemy. This bronze cross was instituted by King Victor Emmanuel III on 19 January 1918 and was also awarded to those were wounded in combat, as Beppe was. The reverse bears a five-pointed star on a background of rays. The obverse has the royal cypher in the upper arm ('VE III' under a crown), 'MERITO DI GVERRA' ('war merit') on the horizontal arms and a Roman sword, point upwards, on oak leaves, on the lower arm.

Medaglia Dell Guerra 1915–1918 (War Medal 1915–1918)

Awarded for participation in World War I. It was instituted on 29 July 1920 and awarded after one year's service in a war zone. Additional war service years were indicated by additional bars attached to the ribbon according to the recipient's war service. These bars are covered with laurel leaves and bear a service year between 1915 and 1918.

The medal's obverse bears the helmeted head of King Victor Emanuel III and around the rim is the text 'GVERRA PER L'VNITA D'ITALIA 1915 1918' ('war for the unity of Italy'). The reverse depicts an upright Victory standing on shields borne by two soldiers. Around the rim is the text 'CONIATA NEL BRONZO NEMICO' ('made from enemy bronze').

Medaglia di Volontario di Guerra 1915–1918 (Medal for the War Volunteer 1915–1918)

Awarded to those who entered the Italian armed forces as volunteers during World War I, as had Beppe. This bronze medal was instituted on 24 May 1924 and has the crowned head of Italia on the obverse as well as the words 'PER L'ITALIA' ('for Italy'). The reverse depicts a naked warrior bearing a shield and a veiled woman behind him. Around the rim run the medal's title and the war's dates: 'VOLONTARIO DI GVERRA MCMXV–MCMXVIII'.

Medaglia a Ricordo dell'Unità d'Italia 1848–1918 (Medal for the Unification of Italy 1848–1918)

Circular bronze medal with laterally pierced loop and ring for suspension; the face with the head of King Victor Emmanuel III facing left, circumscribed 'VITTORIO EMANUELE III RE D'ITALIA'; the reverse inscribed 'UNITÀ D'ITALIA 1848–1918' within a circular laurel wreath. The medal was instituted on 19 January 1922 and awarded to combatants in World War I since it was regarded as the final phase of the Risorgimento (the unification of Italy), which had begun in 1848.

Medaglia Della Vittoria Interalleata (Medal of Allied Victory)

Awarded to Allied participants of World War I. The obverse depicts a winged Victory on a triumphal chariot drawn by four lions, while the reverse has a tower-like structure from which fly two doves. Around the upper rim is the text 'GRANDE GVERRA PER LA CIVILITA' ('the great war for civilisation'), in the middle the war years 'MXMXIV' and 'MXMXVIII' and in the exergue 'AL COMBATIENTI DELLA NAZIONE ALLEATE ED ASSOCIATE' ('to the combatants of the Allied and associated countries'). The medal was instituted on 6 April 1922 and the ribbon bears the same colours as the similar medals awarded to the other Allied countries.

Milton Keynes UK
Ingram Content Group UK Ltd.
UKHW021931160224
437878UK00001B/1